A NEW AUDITOR'S GUIDE TO PLANNING, PERFORMING, AND PRESENTING IT AUDITS

By
Nelson Gibbs (Lead Author), CIA, CISA, CISSP
Divakar Jain, CA, CPA, CISA
Amitesh Joshi, CA, CISA
Surekha Muddamsetti
Sarabjot Singh, CIA, CISA

Disclosure

Copyright © 2010 by The Institute of Internal Auditors Research Foundation (IIARF), 247 Maitland Avenue, Altamonte Springs, Florida 32701-4201. All rights reserved. No part of this publication may be reproduced, stored in a retrieval system, or transmitted in any form by any means — electronic, mechanical, photocopying, recording, or otherwise — without prior written permission of the publisher.

The IIARF publishes this document for informational and educational purposes. This document is intended to provide information, but is not a substitute for legal or accounting advice. The IIARF does not provide such advice and makes no warranty as to any legal or accounting results through its publication of this document. When legal or accounting issues arise, professional assistance should be sought and retained.

The Institute of Internal Auditors' (IIA's) International Professional Practices Framework (IPPF) comprises the full range of existing and developing practice guidance for the profession. The IPPF provides guidance to internal auditors globally and paves the way to world-class internal auditing.

The mission of The IIARF is to expand knowledge and understanding of internal auditing by providing relevant research and educational products to advance the profession globally.

The IIA and The IIARF work in partnership with researchers from around the globe who conduct valuable studies on critical issues affecting today's business world. Much of the content presented in their final reports is a result of IIARF-funded research and prepared as a service to The Foundation and the internal audit profession. Expressed opinions, interpretations, or points of view represent a consensus of the researchers and do not necessarily reflect or represent the official position or policies of The IIA or The IIARF.

ISBN 978-0-89413-685-6
08/10
First Printing

TABLE OF CONTENTS

About the Author v
Preface vii
Introduction ix

Section I: Understanding Technology [IIA Standard 1200] 1
    Chapter 1: What is Internal Auditing and Why is Information
        Technology Special? 5
    Chapter 2: What Technology Should Be Audited? 15

Section II: Planning a Technology Audit [IIA Standard 2200] 31
    Chapter 3: Risk Assessment 35
    Chapter 4: Scoping 51
    Chapter 5: Frameworks and Standards 61

Section III: Performing a Technology Audit [IIA Standard 2300] 81
    Chapter 6: Networks 89
    Chapter 7: Operating Systems 111
    Chapter 8: Databases 129
    Chapter 9: Applications 143
    Chapter 10: Automated Tools: Using Technology to Audit 155

Section IV: Presenting a Technology Audit [IIA Standard 2400] ... 171
    Chapter 11: Interpreting Audit Results 175
    Chapter 12: Writing the Audit Report 177

Appendix 1: Sample Detailed Audit Report 185
Appendix 2: Sample High-level Audit Report 203
Appendix 3: Additional Reading and Related Resources 209
Appendix 4: Contributors 211

Bibliography/References 213

ABOUT THE AUTHOR

Nelson Gibbs, CIA, CISA, CISSP, CISM, CGEIT, is a senior manager in the Internal Audit Transformation group of Deloitte & Touche, where he specializes in technology and works extensively in the financial services industry. He has deep knowledge of information security, IT controls and infrastructure, and business process application risk management. He has more than 16 years' experience in information systems operations and auditing.

Gibbs received an MBA from the University of California at Irvine with an emphasis in information technology. He frequently lectures on business and technology security issues, both in the United States and internationally. He was a member of The Institute of Internal Auditors' (IIA's) global Advanced Technology Committee for three years and currently sits on The IIA's Professional Conferences Committee.

PREFACE

The Institute of Internal Auditors (IIA) has long recognized the importance of technology as a crucial area of focus for the practice of internal auditing. From the massive Systems Assurance and Control research project (first released in 1977 as Systems Auditability and Control) to the current Global Technology Audit Guides (GTAGs) that address timely, topical issues of concern for chief audit executives (CAEs) and internal audit departments, the development of the Guide to the Assessment of IT Risk (GAIT) methodology, and the ongoing presentation of training seminars and conferences with a technology focus, The IIA has consistently demonstrated a commitment to providing internal audit professionals with the skills and knowledge necessary to function effectively in a rapidly changing technology environment.

We hope this guide will help bring together many of the key ideas and topics of the existing materials and guidance provided by The IIA and other recognized leaders in the field. Our goal was to structure them in a format that allows for a general understanding of the IT audit process from beginning to end and how it integrates with the charter and operations of the internal audit function as a whole.

INTRODUCTION

Technology is a business enabler that is used to automate repetitive, tedious, or complex tasks and business processes. It provides immense competitive benefits and capabilities. It also introduces new areas of risk that organizations must identify, quantify, evaluate, and address. It is the role of the internal audit function and the technology auditor to assist management in these activities to improve the control, monitoring, and response to business risks.

This book is intended to provide practical application of academic theory and industry guidance for the process of planning, performing, and presenting a technology audit. It is presented in the context of evaluating, improving, and monitoring business operations and compliance for the purpose of providing assurance regarding the appropriateness, reliability, and effectiveness of the infrastructure environment implemented by an organization. It is primarily based on The IIA's International Professional Practices Framework (IPPF), GTAGs, ISACA's IS Guidelines, Standards, and Procedures, guidance issued by the Committee of Sponsoring Organizations of the Treadway Commission (COSO), and other relevant recognized industry standards and organizations. We hope this book will provide a consistent foundational basis for the auditing of technology related to business risks.

The book provides a broad perspective of the purpose and process of auditing technology. It is not intended to provide detailed information regarding the technical steps necessary to audit a specific technology such as a given operating system version and release or an enterprise resource planning (ERP) implementation, nor is it intended to delve into high-level theoretical or strategic concerns such as the role of internal auditing in an organization's technology strategy. This book is designed to help aspiring and active internal auditors take a step back and understand the general process and activities to be covered when conducting an audit around technology, and how this fits into and supports the goals and objectives of their organization when assessing the technology environment. Accordingly, business processes and their associated risks will only be referenced to illustrate specific points rather than in detail. There are many excellent sources of information for the practice of internal auditing in general and the risks and controls related to specific business processes, a number of which are listed in the Bibliography/References section of this book.

Quite frequently those tasked with auditing technology come from one of two backgrounds: a trained business auditor who is exposed to technology auditing through interest or necessity, or a technology specialist who is moving into the audit profession (commonly through interest or necessity). It is therefore assumed that readers have either a basic understanding of the activities and processes followed by an internal audit professional and are primarily interested in gaining greater knowledge regarding specific areas of technology to enhance their effectiveness as auditors, or are knowledgeable about technology and require a better understanding of the audit process in the context of their existing areas of experience. Consequently some sections of this guide may appear more or less elementary to readers, depending on their existing knowledge and history.

Throughout the book we use a simplified four-layer technology model consisting of networks, operating systems, databases, and applications, and three major areas of technology processes: operations, security, and change management. This reference model and its use are described in greater detail in Sections I and II. Each technical chapter presents a sample of three common risks (one for each process) inherent in that specific technology layer along with two or three sample control activities for each risk that might be found in a typical IT environment. These examples are presented for illustrative purposes only and are not comprehensive or relevant to every environment. Chapters addressing the audit process as it relates to the audit of technology are presented with some historical context and basic explanations of the rationale and approach behind the methods to help those less familiar with auditing to begin to build a vocabulary and understanding of the world of internal auditing.

Other texts and approaches use varying numbers of IT activities, technologies and areas of focus for an audit. This book is not intended to contradict or replace those models; rather it is intended to provide an easily understandable concept of a technology environment that can be applied in a majority of organizations with little modification while addressing the majority of the implemented systems and processes. It is not the granularity of each item that provides for a successful audit, but rather the comprehensiveness of the approach and the understanding of its limitations that determines whether or not an IT audit delivers value to an organization. Understanding the purpose of a particular audit and the intended use of the results will go further toward providing a successful audit for an organization than diligently following a checklist that is comprehensive nevertheless. Different organizations with different technologies face differing risks and have individual risk appetites. Each audit will be unique to each organization and the scoping and planning

Introduction

activities require as much effort and thought as goes into performing the fieldwork.

This book is organized into four main sections: Section I, "Understanding Technology in the Context of Internal Auditing," Section II, "Planning a Technology Audit," Section III, "Performing a Technology Audit," and Section IV, "Presenting a Technology Audit." Each section is broken up into chapters that address a specific concept or technology related to the section topic necessary to perform a reasonable IT audit. The structure is directly related to The IIA's Performance Standards 2200: "Engagement Planning," 2300: "Performing the Engagement," and 2400: "Communicating Results." The book also contains a detailed bibliography and reference section that provides a listing of useful materials that can be used for further research and learning.

Information technology is a highly dynamic and rapidly changing environment. IT auditors must stay current with the latest tools, technologies, and trends to maintain a reasonable understanding of the environment, and may need to do additional detailed research in preparation for specific audits. We hope readers find this book valuable and useful on their journey to developing or improving their audit skills.

Section I
Understanding Technology

IIA Standard 1200 – Proficiency and Due Professional Care
Engagements must be performed with proficiency and due professional care.

1210 – Proficiency
Internal auditors must possess the knowledge, skills, and other competencies needed to perform their individual responsibilities. The internal audit activity collectively must possess or obtain the knowledge, skills, and other competencies needed to perform its responsibilities.

Interpretation:
Knowledge, skills, and other competencies is a collective term that refers to the professional proficiency required of internal auditors to effectively carry out their professional responsibilities. Internal auditors are encouraged to demonstrate their proficiency by obtaining appropriate professional certifications and qualifications, such as the Certified Internal Auditor designation and other designations offered by The Institute of Internal Auditors and other appropriate professional organizations.

> **1210.A1** – The chief audit executive must obtain competent advice and assistance if the internal auditors lack the knowledge, skills, or other competencies needed to perform all or part of the engagement.
>
> **1210.A2** – Internal auditors must have sufficient knowledge to evaluate the risk of fraud and the manner in which it is managed by the organization, but are not expected to have the expertise of a person whose primary responsibility is detecting and investigating fraud.
>
> **1210.A3** – Internal auditors must have sufficient knowledge of key information technology risks and controls and available technology-based audit techniques to perform their assigned work. However, not all internal auditors are expected to have the expertise of an internal auditor whose primary responsibility is information technology auditing.

1210.C1 – The chief audit executive must decline the consulting engagement or obtain competent advice and assistance if the internal auditors lack the knowledge, skills, or other competencies needed to perform all or part of the engagement.

1220 – Due Professional Care
Internal auditors must apply the care and skill expected of a reasonably prudent and competent internal auditor. Due professional care does not imply infallibility.

1220.A1 – Internal auditors must exercise due professional care by considering the:

- Extent of work needed to achieve the engagement's objectives;
- Relative complexity, materiality, or significance of matters to which assurance procedures are applied;
- Adequacy and effectiveness of governance, risk management, and control processes;
- Probability of significant errors, fraud, or noncompliance; and
- Cost of assurance in relation to potential benefits.

1220.A2 – In exercising due professional care internal auditors must consider the use of technology-based audit and other data analysis techniques.

1220.A3 – Internal auditors must be alert to the significant risks that might affect objectives, operations, or resources. However, assurance procedures alone, even when performed with due professional care, do not guarantee that all significant risks will be identified.

1220.C1 – Internal auditors must exercise due professional care during a consulting engagement by considering the:
- Needs and expectations of clients, including the nature, timing, and communication of engagement results;
- Relative complexity and extent of work needed to achieve the engagement's objectives; and
- Cost of the consulting engagement in relation to potential benefits.

1230 – Continuing Professional Development
Internal auditors must enhance their knowledge, skills, and other competencies through continuing professional development.

Section I: Understanding Technology

CHAPTER 1

WHAT IS INTERNAL AUDITING AND WHY IS INFORMATION TECHNOLOGY SPECIAL?

Overview

Internal auditing can be defined as an evaluation of an organization, system, or process. Audits help to ascertain the reliability and validity of information, and also provide an assessment of the system's internal control. In an audit, a conclusion is expressed on the subject being evaluated based on work performed on a selective basis. Statistical sampling is often used in audits due to practical constraints. As a result, an audit seeks to provide only reasonable assurance that the work reviewed substantially mitigates the risks identified. Audits were traditionally associated with gaining information about the financial records of an organization or business. However, recently they have begun to encompass subjects as diverse as environmental concerns, corporate social responsibility, and information systems.

In financial accounting, an audit is an independent assessment of the fairness of an organization's financial statements as presented by its management, providing reasonable but not absolute assurance. It is performed by competent, independent, and objective persons known as auditors or accountants who then issue a report on the results of the audit. Auditors are required to adhere to generally accepted standards set by governing bodies that regulate businesses. In summary, financial audits provide assurance for interested parties that such statements present "fairly" an organization's financial condition and results of operations.

In management accounting, the focus is on using financial data and other internal information in a forward looking and more consultative fashion to assist management in the operation of the organization. An audit in this environment has a more broad and flexible scope and purpose when compared to a financial audit. The work should still be performed by competent, independent, and objective professionals, but it is frequently at the direction of, or in conjunction with, the management of the organizations rather than entirely independent.

An evaluation and examination of the controls within an IT environment or system is commonly termed an information technology audit, or information systems audit. IT audit is the process of collecting and evaluating evidence of an organization's information systems, practices, and operations. The evaluation of obtained evidence determines whether the information systems are safeguarding assets, maintaining data integrity, and operating effectively and efficiently to achieve the organization's goals and objectives. These reviews may be performed as part of a broader review, such as a financial statement audit, operational audit, compliance audit, etc. Increasingly, with government regulations such as the U.S. Sarbanes-Oxley Act of 2002, Clause 49 in India, or J-SOX in Japan, IT audits are an important tool used by external stakeholders to assess the strength of an organization's IT control structure and financial reporting integrity.

History

In the 1950s, analysis of an entity's IT infrastructure was commonly known as an EDP audit. EDP stands for electronic data processing, the original term for computer technology applied to business use and record keeping. EDP auditing developed largely as a result of the rise in technology in accounting systems, the need for IT control, and the impact of computers on the ability to perform attestation services. Today, however, the term "IT audit" is more widely used. An IT audit may involve examining any or all IT business processes, systems, components, and data that processes or integrates with an organization's business activities or financial systems. The examinations review the operating effectiveness of controls and compliance with corporate policies.

The introduction of computer technology into accounting systems changed the way data was stored, retrieved, and controlled. Up until the mid-1960s, the audit profession was still auditing around the computer. At that time, only mainframe computers were used and few people had the skills and abilities to program computers. This began to change in the mid-1960s with the introduction of new, smaller, and less expensive computers. This increased the use of computers in businesses and with it came the need for auditors to become familiar with EDP concepts in business. Along with the increase in computer use came the rise of different types of accounting systems. In 1977, the first edition of Control Objectives was published. This publication is now known as

Chapter 1: What is Internal Auditing and Why is IT Special?

Control Objectives for Information and related Technology (COBIT). COBIT, as used later in the Frameworks and Standards section, is a set of generally accepted IT control objectives. The period from the late 1960s through today has seen rapid changes in technology from the microcomputer and networking to the Internet, and with these changes came some major events that changed IT auditing forever.

The formation and rise in popularity of the Internet and e-commerce has had significant influences on the growth of IT audit. Evolution of new technologies has had an impact on business around the world and therefore has impacted the audit profession as well. Some of the significant technology impacts on the business environment over the past few years include:

- More organizations are going beyond traditional ERP solutions and incorporating business intelligence solutions, data warehousing, and data mining solutions.

- Typical computerized applications from the 1990s onward incorporate, and are developed using, advanced methodologies and techniques that are often decentralized and have distributed databases.

- Applications are moving from client-server technology to web-based architecture models.

- More organizations are linking their systems with external suppliers and/or customers to create complex, interdependent supply chain mechanisms.

- Online sales are increasing.

- There is an increase in the development and adoption of standards to improve corporate governance, customer service, and security.

- Beginning in 2009, the U.S. Securities and Exchange Commission (SEC) adopted a rule requiring companies to file their financial statements in eXtensible Business Reporting Language (XBRL).

- The adoption of International Financial Reporting Standards (IFRS) over the next several years in new geographies such as Asia and the United States.

- Remote computing by employees and business partners using technologies such as wireless is proliferating.

As computer technology has advanced, organizations have become increasingly dependent on computerized information systems to carry out their operations and to process, maintain, and report essential information. As a consequence, the reliability of computerized data and the systems that process, maintain, and report these data is a major concern to organizations. IT auditors evaluate the reliability of computer-generated data supporting financial statements and analyze specific programs and their outcomes. In addition, they examine the adequacy of controls in information systems and related operations to help ensure system effectiveness. IT auditing helps organizations and individuals determine whether identified risks have been mitigated, corporate policies and procedures are implemented as designed, and systems can be relied upon. An organization that has a well-controlled IT environment is better suited to achieve interrelated objectives that are supported, such as integrity of data for financial statement reporting, efficiency of technology for operational quality, and compliance with laws and regulations.

Advancements in IT have increased the complexities of performing an audit. For example, in regard to access, mainframe systems primarily had centralized privileged system access. However, with newer distributed systems, privileged system access minimally will exist at the network, operating system, database, and application level. Changes in technology, such as the development of "cloud computing," the migration of network addressing from IP v4 to IP v6, the evolution of "green computing," and the rapid pace of change in the computing environment and the business world in general, combine to make IT auditing a more relevant discipline and profession than ever before.

Purpose

IT auditing generally involves collecting and evaluating evidence to determine whether a computer system has been designed to maintain data integrity, safeguard assets, and dispense information to authorized parties, as well as to help determine whether organizational goals are being achieved effectively and resources used efficiently. An IT audit's agenda can usually be summarized by the following questions:

- Will the information in the systems be disclosed only to authorized users (confidentiality)?

Chapter 1: What is Internal Auditing and Why is IT Special?

- Will the information provided by the system be accurate, reliable, and timely (integrity)?

- Will the organization's computer systems and information be available for the business at all times when required (availability)?

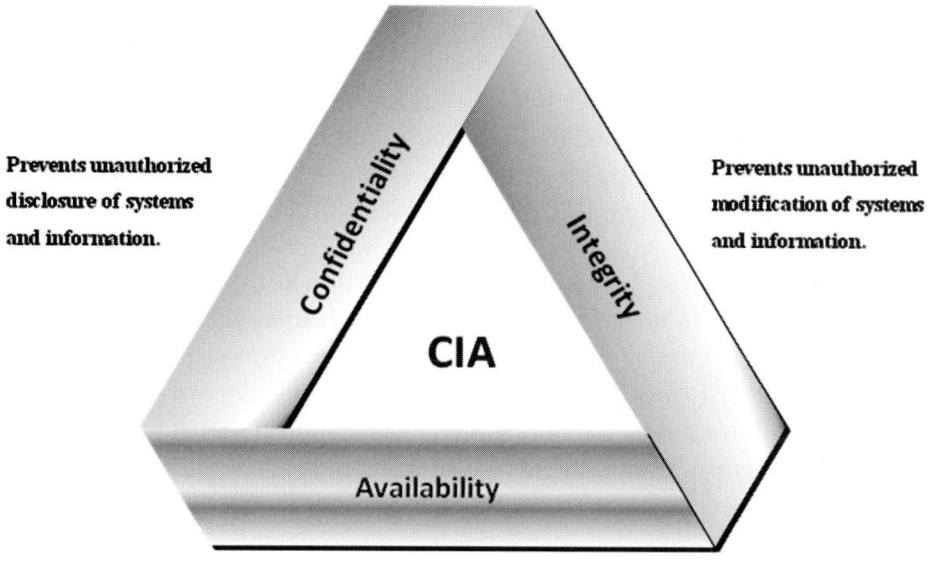

An effective information system leads the organization to achieve its objectives, and an efficient information system uses minimum resources in achieving the required objectives. An IT auditor should become familiar with the characteristics of users of the information system and the decision-making environment in the organization being audited while evaluating the effectiveness of any system. The IT audit focuses on determining risks that are relevant to information assets and assessing controls to reduce or mitigate these risks. By implementing controls, the effect of risks can be minimized, but not completely eliminated.

Although there are many common taxonomies used to identify the boundaries of various IT audit approaches, it is convenient to categorize all IT audits into two broad types: "general control review" audits or "application control review" audits. This approach is the one used throughout much of this book. Using this simplified approach, general computer controls (GCCs) are pervasive throughout the IT environment and support numerous activities, but do not link directly to any specific business process or transaction. Application controls generally relate to business transactions or processes and include specific technical configuration or security settings within a particular system, such as a general ledger application. As an example, a GCC could apply to the procedure for patching the code used to operate a network router that supports all information movement throughout an organization, while an application control might control which general ledger accounts can be posted to manually.

Auditors must plan and conduct the audit to limit their audit risk (the risk of reaching an incorrect conclusion based on the audit findings) to an acceptable level. To help achieve this objective, they should generally perform the following steps:

- **Obtain an understanding of the organization and its environment:** Understanding the organization and its environment helps to assess the risk to the organization and determine the scope of the audit. The auditors' understanding should include information on the nature of the entity, management, governance, objectives and strategies, and business processes.

- **Identify risks:** The auditors should evaluate an organization's business risks (threats to the organization's ability to achieve its objectives). Business risks can be financial, operational, or compliance-related in nature. Risks evolve over time due to many factors such as new personnel, new or restructured information systems, corporate restructuring, new legislation, and rapid growth, to name a few.

- **Evaluate the organization's response to those risks:** Once the auditors have evaluated the organization's response to the assessed risks, they should obtain evidence of management's actions to address those risks. The organization's response (or lack thereof) to any business risks will impact the auditors' assessed level of audit risk.

- **Assess the risk of not meeting objectives:** Based on the knowledge obtained in evaluating the organization's responses to business risks, the auditors then assess the risk of not meeting the objectives and determine specific audit procedures that are necessary based on that risk assessment.

Chapter 1: What is Internal Auditing and Why is IT Special?

- **Evaluate results and issue an audit report:** At this level, the auditors should determine whether the assessments of risks were appropriate and sufficient evidence was obtained. They will issue an audit report based on their findings to management and interested parties.

COSO's enterprise risk management (ERM) has encouraged organizations to build a comprehensive risk strategy into their business operations and spurred auditors to move from a primarily control-based approach to a predominantly risk-based approach. One major area of enterprise risk that internal auditors must understand is how IT affects their organization within the context of COSO's *Enterprise Risk Management – Integrated Framework*. IT is intertwined with all eight components of COSO's ERM framework — as both a source of risk and a risk management tool. Auditors also can add substantial value to the organization by providing advice on using IT to develop a sound ERM program. Auditors must first understand how technology impacts each component of the ERM framework.

1. **Internal Environment:** The internal environment sets the overall tone of the organization's response to risk and provides an actionable basis for all other components of COSO's ERM framework. It includes the organization's ethical values, risk appetite, ERM philosophy, and the competence and development of its employees, as well as how the organization views risk and implements controls. These parameters of organizational control and behavior may be referred to as entity-level controls as they are often defined at the top of the organization, but are pervasive at all levels. Risk appetite is the level of risk that an organization is willing to accept, which affects its choice of IT, e-commerce strategy, and use of emerging technologies. Such technology decisions not only change the organization's risks, but also make them more complex. For example, the moment an organization engages in e-commerce, it becomes global, even if its operations are geographically confined to one country. As a result, organizations that sell products and services online must address a host of security, confidentiality, and privacy risks and technology compatibility issues that they might not face if they only conducted business through traditional retail channels.

2. **Objective Setting:** According to COSO's ERM, the organization's mission and risk appetite drive its objective-setting process, which defines high-level strategic objectives and the corresponding operating, financial reporting, and compliance objectives needed to accomplish them. Strategic objectives affect the organization's selected IT infrastructure

and risk level. IT, however, influences organizational objectives in a sort of "chicken and egg" manner: it can drive as well as enable organizational strategy. But IT also generates new risks that may require technology solutions. For example, organizations that use e-mail to communicate and manage knowledge must establish appropriate IT protocols, passwords, and authentication procedures to keep messages secure. Moreover, IT is critical to using operational assets effectively and helping to ensure the integrity and reliability of the organization's financial reporting system.

3. **Event Identification:** COSO ERM highlights the unique role that IT plays in identifying events or incidents that may affect the organization's ability to achieve its objectives. Events may be characterized as negative risks or positive opportunities. COSO contends that IT is the only factor that can be viewed as an external or internal event, while functioning as an "environmental scanner" to identify other events.

    When viewing IT as an external event, an organization must consider the positive and negative effects that its e-commerce environment and new technology can have on the business. Although new technologies and services can enhance the availability of data and lower infrastructure costs, they also can increase demand for technology-based services and cause service interruptions. These advances also can disrupt the organization's business model and relationships with suppliers, customers, and other business partners.

    When viewing IT as an internal event, an organization must determine how volume volatility, data integrity, data and system availability, and system selection, development, deployment, and maintenance may affect its operations. These advances also can disrupt the organization's processes, control structure, and employees.

4. **Risk Assessment:** COSO's ERM characterizes risk assessment as a continuous process of estimating the likelihood of potential events and their impact on the organization. Likelihood is the possibility or probability that an event will occur, while impact is the outcome of the event (e.g., financial, operational, or compliance outcome). New technologies and e-commerce have made IT a significant and evolving source of business risk that must be assessed. Estimates of the likelihood and impact associated with IT risk may change frequently as technology changes and systems become increasingly integrated across organizations and their business partners. For example, new viruses emerge each day with the

potential to interrupt or shut down an organization's operations and any integrated system.

However, IT also can be a valuable risk-assessment tool. For example, auditors can mine internal, external, and industry benchmarking data to estimate the likelihood and impact of an event. Tools such as simulation, modeling, stress testing, scenario analysis, and optimization can estimate the various financial impacts of different time horizons and probability models.

5. **Risk Response:** Following the risk assessment phase, COSO's ERM discusses the need for an appropriate organizational risk response to help ensure that the residual risk is within the acceptable risk-tolerance level. Residual risk is the risk that remains after considering the organization's risk response. Remember, not all risks can be eliminated.

    Organizations may select one of several responses to IT risk — avoidance, sharing, reduction, or acceptance. To avoid IT risks, an organization may minimize IT usage, steer clear of e-commerce and emerging technologies, and reduce the number of IT contact points with the outside world. The organization may opt to share the risks by augmenting its standard insurance with supplemental insurance that covers network-related incidents and other IT risks that are not part of their policy's property, commercial general liability, and crime coverage. If the organization decides to reduce IT risks, internal auditors must make sure strong IT controls that can alter the organization's risk profile are established. Finally, if an organization determines that the inherent IT risks are within its risk-tolerance level, no action is required. Instead, the organization would simply factor those risks into the level of "self-insured risk" it is willing to assume.

    When selecting a risk response, the organization must analyze the costs and benefits of reducing the likelihood and impact of the risk. This cost-benefit analysis should be conducted from a portfolio viewpoint that examines interrelated risks, because risks across the organization may counterbalance or exacerbate each other.

6. **Control Activities:** COSO's ERM describes control activities as the policies, procedures, processes, and monitoring mechanisms that help ensure the selected risk responses are in place and determined appropriately. The audit function can play a pivotal role by helping the organization define manual and IT controls to prevent, detect, and correct potential

issues. Built-in preventive IT controls in the form of input edit checks can help ensure that transactions are complete, accurate, authorized, and valid. Similarly, organizations must confirm and validate the existence and operating effectiveness of general and application controls. This is especially true after a new system is implemented because built-in access controls are often not fully deployed in order to get the system up and running as quickly as possible, or powerful access required to implement the new system may not be turned off or removed after implementation.

7. **Information and Communication:** IT is the basis of the COSO ERM information and communication component. Reliable, timely information is needed to identify, analyze, and respond to risks. ERP systems, in conjunction with integrated data warehouses, can collect, process, and seamlessly distribute vast amounts of internal and external data for ERM in a short time. IT also can be used to communicate needed information across all levels of the organization. Auditors can help ensure that ERP and other systems are fully integrated so that information flows accurately and quickly — vertically, horizontally, upstream, and downstream — throughout the organization. This integration can prevent organizations from being bogged down by information fragmentation or bottlenecks and allow decision makers to keep up with the rate of change in the organization's internal and external environments.

8. **Monitoring:** COSO's ERM framework considers the monitoring function to be critical for any effective ERM implementation. In today's rapidly changing business environment, the organization's ERM plan must be reviewed regularly to help ensure that the organization is always controlling risk effectively. This requires ongoing monitoring that is real-time, dynamic, and embedded in the organization. For example, to maintain segregation of duties, any changes to user access privileges should be logged automatically for further review.

The rapid pace of IT and organizational change places greater pressure on auditors to pay close attention to how IT impacts their organization's ERM process. Auditors must understand the organization's systems, infrastructure, programs, processes, and constituents; record and evaluate controls over critical and sensitive information; assess monitoring procedures; and obtain external assurances.

CHAPTER 2

WHAT TECHNOLOGY SHOULD BE AUDITED?

When determining what technology should be audited, there is no "right" answer. A poor choice is to begin with a checklist for a particular technology and execute the test steps without first understanding the overall audit scope and related risks and objectives. After going through the process outlined in the previous chapter to identify the risks and objectives for a particular audit, this chapter focuses on some specific areas of the technology process that should be considered within that scope in addition to the specific technology itself:

- IT Strategy
- Personnel Management
- Sourcing Practices
- Business Continuity and Disaster Recovery
- Change Management
- User Provisioning and Segregation of Duties
- Configuration Management
- Operations
- Security
- Monitoring

This is not a comprehensive listing of areas to be tested but is rather a collection of commonly encountered topics relevant to a wide variety of IT audits. It can be used as a general starting point to identify some of the more likely elements that may need to be considered during the course of developing an audit work program or performing an audit. Because these topics are complex processes in and of themselves, they will be designed and performed differently across organizations. However, there should be a well-defined and understood process in place (preferably documented) that the IT auditor can use as a guide for his or her environment when developing an audit program. These "indigenous" practices should be considered along with recognized industry practices and frameworks to help guide the auditor to a comprehensive audit process that measures both the client's compliance with expected practices and the organization's deployment of the best practices for their environment.

This chapter also briefly addresses the concepts of an integrated audit and continuous auditing, two very effective approaches to an audit of technology, providing possible considerations of the "how" for an IT audit. Excellent guidance for all of these topics can be found throughout The IIA's GTAG series.

IT Strategy

Strategic planning from an information systems standpoint relates to the long-term direction an organization wants to take in leveraging IT for improving its business processes. Under the responsibility of top management, factors to consider include identifying cost-effective IT solutions in addressing problems and opportunities that confront the organization, and developing action plans for identifying and acquiring needed resources.

When developing IT strategic plans, organizations should evaluate whether the plans are fully aligned and consistent with the overall organizational goals and objectives. Information technology departmental management, along with the IT steering committee and the strategy committee, play a key role in the development and implementation of these plans. Effective IT strategic planning involves consideration of the organization's demand for IT and its IT supply capacity. Determining IT demand involves a systematic consideration of the organization's strategic intentions, how these translate into specific objectives and business initiatives, and what IT capabilities will be needed to support these objectives and initiatives. For example, if the organization is anticipating substantial growth or acquisition, the IT capabilities must have resource capacity for these future activities. Conversely, if the organization is divesting businesses, increased consideration may be focused on how data assets are protected as IT functionality (and perhaps systems) are carved out of the existing organization. In assessing IT capabilities, the existing system's portfolio should be reviewed in terms of functional fit, cost, and risk. IT supply planning involves assessing the organization's technical IT infrastructure and key support processes to determine whether expansion or improvement is necessary. It is important that the strategic planning process encompasses not just the delivery of new systems and technology, but considers the returns being achieved from investment in existing IT infrastructure.

Personnel Management

Personnel management relates to organizational policies and procedures for hiring, promotion, retention, training, and termination. The effectiveness of these activities as they relate to the IT functions can impact the quality of staff and the effective performance of IT duties, and potentially impact related controls (e.g., successful removal of access from terminated personnel). An organization's hiring practices are important for helping ensure that appropriately skilled personnel are hired and the organization is in compliance with legal recruitment requirements.

Sourcing Practices

Sourcing practices relate to the way in which the organization will obtain the IT functions required to support the business. Organizations can perform all of the IT functions in-house (known as "insourcing") in a centralized fashion, or outsource some or all functions across the globe. The sourcing strategy should consider each IT function and determine which approach allows them to meet the overall organizational goals.

Delivery of IT functions can include:

- **Insourced** — Fully performed by the organization's staff.
- **Outsourced** — Fully performed by the vendor's staff.
- **Hybrid** — Performed by a mix of the organization's and vendor's staff.

IT functions can be performed across the globe, taking advantage of time zones and differing labor rates, and can include:

- **Onsite** — Personnel work onsite in the IT department.
- **Offsite** — Personnel work at a remote location in the same geographical area.
- **Offshore** — Personnel work at a remote location in a different geographic region.

The organization should evaluate its IT functions and determine the most appropriate way to deliver these services and capabilities, giving consideration to:

- Is this a core function for the organization?

- Does this function have specific knowledge, processes, and personnel that are critical to meeting its goals and objectives, and that cannot be replicated externally or in another location?

- Can this function be performed by another party or in another location for the same or lower price, with the same or higher quality, and without increasing risk?

- Does the organization have experience managing third parties or using remote/offshore locations to execute IT or business functions?

- For functions that are outsourced, can we obtain evidence of the effectiveness of their control structure (e.g., Type II SAS70 report, etc.)?

As a note, while efficiencies can be gained through outsourced arrangements, careful consideration of these agreements should be given as, in many instances, they result in moving some level of an organization's IT controls to outside parties. Therefore, at a minimum, agreements must include comprehensive service-level agreements, methods used to control the inappropriate dissemination of privileged information and system access by the outsourcers' staff, and a right-to-audit clause in the contract.

Business Continuity/Disaster Recovery

Business Continuity Planning (BCP) and Disaster Recovery Planning (DRP) are processes that help organizations prepare for disruptive events, ranging from natural disasters such as a hurricane to localized events such as a power outage. Generally, a high-level strategic executive should be responsible for overseeing those involved with documenting potential events, defining a comprehensive response, overseeing mock tests for the defined responses, and modifying those plans accordingly to help ensure all areas of the business are adequately addressed throughout an integrated BCP/DRP program. Each business area will best understand and be able to contribute its specific needs to a comprehensive recovery program. However, the IT department should be involved with many of the areas because they are responsible for providing support functions to almost all of the business operations.

DR is the process by which business resumes after a disruptive event, generally through restoring critical information and systems. The event could include anything from an earthquake to malfunctioning software caused by a computer virus. BCP suggests a more comprehensive approach to ensuring the organization is able to continue the core business operations over time, not only after a natural calamity, but also in the event of smaller disruptions, such as the departure of key personnel, supply chain partner issues, etc. Despite these distinctions, the two terms are often married under the acronym BCP/DR because of their many common considerations.

BCP/DR plans should detail how employees will communicate, where they will go, and how they will continue to perform their duties. The details can vary greatly, depending on the size and scope of an organization and the manner in which it operates. For some businesses, issues such as supply chain logistics are most crucial and are the focus of the plan. For others, IT may play a more pivotal role, and the BCP/DR plan may have more of a focus on systems recovery. Neither element can be ignored, and physical, IT, and human resources plans cannot be developed in isolation. While the scope of IT audit might include review of a BCP or DR, the broader scope invariably involves other types of audits (operational, etc.). For example, the IT audit may focus more closely on how data is retrieved, restored, and available to personnel, while an operational component of the audit may focus more closely on how disasters are communicated, how employees are kept safe, and how they continue paying personnel.

Change Management

The change process itself consists of a series of subprocesses encompassing areas such as:

- Change Request.
- Change Review.
- Change Development.
- Change Testing.
- Change Approval.
- Change Deployment.
- Post-change Follow-up and Validation.

The change management process begins with requesting proposed changes to systems. As changes to the IT environment (whether to infrastructure items such as databases or to application code to modify the processing of transactions) can have a major impact on the overall integrity of the environment, any change can pose a significant risk to the organization. For this purpose, there should be a methodology for prioritizing and approving system change requests. Change requests may be initiated from users, operational staff, or system development/maintenance staff. Authorization should be obtained from appropriate stakeholders, which can include the business process owners and IT personnel. For example, for acquired systems, a vendor may distribute periodic updates, patches, or new release levels of the software. Changes of this type are frequently referred to as "patch management," but should follow a defined and documented process just as any other change to a system as they present the same types of risks and can have the same potential impacts on the environment if not managed correctly. User and systems management should review such changes and determine whether they are appropriate for the organization and whether or not they will negatively affect existing systems.

Requests to make system modifications should be communicated via a documented system that could include a formal change tracking system or, in some cases, a less sophisticated method, such as hard copy change request forms, memos, or e-mail. The request generally includes, at a minimum, the requestor's name, date of the request, date the change is needed, priority of the request, a thorough description of the change request, testing detail, a description of any anticipated effects on other systems or programs, and evidence that the request has been approved and reviewed by authorized personnel. The change request could also provide a reason for the change, a cost justification analysis, and expected benefits. Before the change is migrated to the production environment, it should be subject to testing by relevant stakeholders. For example, if an operating system patch is applied, testing may be performed by IT personnel in a test environment to help ensure it is functioning as anticipated and the existing functionality (including the functioning of security) has not been negatively impacted. If an upgrade to a database or application were applied, in addition to any testing performed by IT personnel, it may be appropriate for the users to perform testing to help ensure that the new application functionality and/or database structure functions as intended and existing functionality has not been negatively impacted. The organization's policies and procedures for change requirements should be explicitly documented and should specify the requirements for each type of change.

Change requests should be in a format that helps ensure all changes are considered for action and that allow management to easily track the status of the request. This is usually accomplished by assigning a unique control number to each request and entering the change request information into a computerized system, but it also can be performed manually.

User Provisioning and Segregation of Duties (SOD)

User provisioning refers to the process of assigning, modifying, and removing user access to systems based on current job responsibilities. Users are generally assigned new access when they join the organization or if they switch job responsibilities. They generally have their access *modified* within a particular system when changing job responsibilities within the organization, or *removed* when they change job responsibilities within the organization, resign, or, in the case of contractors, their assignment ends.

The methods that organizations employ to manage this process are varied, but most use either manual (e.g., the user's manager manually notifies the various system administrators to change access) or automated (e.g., the human resources system automatically disables network access on the termination date via an automated process).

The organization should have a defined process for their user provisioning activities. The defined process should include guidance regarding how access changes are requested, the level of detail that is specified in the change request, and who is authorized to approve such changes. When assigning new systems access, it is important to specify a sufficient level of detail. For example, a new user request for a financial system that states "add access *like* John Doe" can be problematic in that the approver might assume incorrectly what type of access the existing person really has. One approach to addressing this issue is to create "roles" rather than "users" for systems. In using role-based access control, each job or role within an organization (e.g., finance supervisor or HR specialist) has a defined set of tasks or activities to perform, and the rights or authorities necessary to access or perform those tasks are collected together as a "role," which is then assigned to a user rather than the individual rights being assigned to each user. This simplifies the need to administer individual users separately, aids in ensuring conflicts related to segregation of duties are considered, and allows a change in job responsibilities to be easily applied to all affected users with a single change to the role template. A critical concept to keep in mind when looking at the user provisioning process is that the creation and assignment of user capabilities should be performed by a function independent of the affected business unit to reduce the risk of fraud, enforce segregation of duties, and help ensure that appropriately trained and knowledgeable individuals are the only people making changes to a system.

Many organizations struggle with keeping system access current based on job responsibilities. In addition to the preventative control of approving new and modified systems access, it is often wise to implement a detective control in the form of periodically reviewing system access to help ensure it remains appropriate based on job responsibilities. This type of review should include a sufficiently detailed report with which to review access and should be reviewed by a relevant process owner (e.g., controller for super user access within a general ledger application). As important as keeping appropriate access current and periodically reviewed is the timely removal of access when a user changes job roles or separates from the organization. Such removal is critical to prevent unauthorized access, particularly to sensitive or valuable information.

Job titles and organizational structures vary greatly from one organization to another, depending on the size and nature of the business. However, it is important for an IT auditor to obtain information to assess the relationship among various job functions, responsibilities, and authorities in determining if adequate SOD is in place. SOD avoids the possibility that a single person could be responsible for functions such that errors or misappropriations could occur and not be detected timely in the normal course of business processes. For example, an organization might not want a system administrator to review audit logs that include their own activities. Another example might include users who can create vendors, approve invoices, and print checks. SOD is an important means by which fraudulent and/or malicious acts can be discouraged and prevented.

SOD conflicts within a particular organization should be explicitly documented. Ideally, this occurs before creating roles within applications such that any inherent SOD conflicts (roles that, by default, contain SOD conflicts) can be modified before assigning those roles to users. From a preventative perspective, SOD conflicts should be evaluated before assigning access, either through an inherent SOD conflict as mentioned above or through the assignment of multiple roles that cause a SOD conflict. In addition, the periodic review of access mentioned above within the user provisioning description can be used to review any potential SOD conflicts not previously detected. In conjunction with segregating conflicting job roles within the IT function, it is critically important to make sure there are no user IDs shared by multiple users, as this can cause a segregation-of-duties conflict when IDs with separate role responsibilities are used by a single user (this is known as "aggregation" and should be avoided). Sharing IDs also eliminates one of the key purposes of the use of unique IDs, which is the ability to determine who is accountable for actions taken within the system. Where SOD conflicts are unavoidable due to business

Chapter 2: What Technology Should Be Audited?

constraints, the specific roles and users should be identified as high risk, and mitigating controls (most commonly monitoring in nature) should be designed and regularly tested.

This segregation is critically important for a strong IT control environment, as inappropriate or poorly tested changes are often the root cause of system disruptions or outages at organizations. Conversely, business areas often have numerous segregation-of-duties controls implemented through specific application system access privileges. Understanding of these controls and responsibility for their enforcement generally resides in the respective business unit, with monitoring assistance provided by IT (e.g., user access listings). Similar to IT segregation of duties, business application systems access controls are often the subject of an integrated audit (defined in more detail later in this chapter).

As you conduct IT audits, you may find a significant challenge in many large organizations, because segregation of duties control sustainability is reacting to the movement of individuals and modifying their system access timely as they change job roles. Changes in personnel or roles often require corresponding changes to systems. This challenge requires optimal coordination between HR, IT, and the business units to manage the risk effectively.

Configuration Management

Configuration management refers to creation of a baseline and change management process for configurable settings within the various IT systems. These settings can include security-related items, such as password parameters and auditing configuration, and application configuration, such as three-way matching or chart of accounts settings.

The initial baseline for these settings is similar to creating documented policies within an organization. It serves to instruct process owners of management's intent when configuring systems. It also serves as a guide when replicating well-controlled environments.

Configuration management is inextricably linked to the overall change management process. When implementing new systems, the systems should be reviewed to help ensure they comply with existing baseline settings. When modifying an existing system, not only does the newly modified system need to be compared to the baseline settings while being tested in the test environment, but an assessment needs to be performed to determine whether any additional settings need to be added to the baseline configuration (e.g., a newly updated system might contain a newly created parameter, which must be considered). For these reasons, many organizations mandate that configuration changes be incorporated into their overall change control process to help ensure they are reviewed, tested, and approved in accordance with the organization's procedures and policies.

There are some automated tools that can capture a snapshot of system configurations. These tools are useful not just in assisting with documenting current configuration, but also creating alerts when key configuration settings are modified. This latter portion of the functionality may serve as a key control in mitigating risks related to modification of such settings.

Operations

Operations refers to the day-to-day activities of the IT function and encompasses such activities as job scheduling (the processing of computing activities that are automated and occur at predefined times of the day, such as a backup that occurs overnight), problem management (sometimes also referred to as the helpdesk), incident management, daily maintenance and updating of systems, and all of the other routine procedures that are carried out by the IT department. Operations also can include the design and implementation of computing environments, and the budgeting, management, and oversight of the IT function itself.

Operations can be performed solely in-house, co-sourced with specialist vendors, or outsourced entirely to IT service organizations. However the operations are handled within an organization, there should be documented policies, processes, and procedures to provide guidance to those responsible for the IT services needed by the organization.

Security

Security can be broken into two broad categories: logical and physical. Physical security encompasses access to, and the protection of, tangible items such as computer hardware, specific locations such as a data center, employees such as IT operations staff, and other physical objects. Logical security refers to the protection of access to non-physical elements such as computer files, system activities, areas of computer networks, and other intangible aspects of an IT environment through the use of software safeguards such as access controls, authentication mechanisms, authorization rights, and systems auditing. Logical security typically includes both configuration elements such as role-based access controls and device-based elements such as firewalls and intrusion prevention systems. IT security is a component in every aspect of the IT environment and is commonly audited both as a specific subject in its own right and as an element of other audits as well.

Monitoring

The term "monitoring" can be used to describe two different things. The first is monitoring the actual IT environment. An example is monitoring the health of the network to ensure availability. Another type of monitoring entails monitoring controls for effective operation. An example of this type of monitoring might include reviewing audit logs of network traffic for the effectiveness of the firewall configuration.

For the first type of monitoring, processes should be defined for conditions that support the effective operation of the system. Examples of this type of monitoring might include network monitoring, application batch job monitoring, and data backup monitoring. The purpose in monitoring these areas includes helping to ensure system availability, complete and timely recording of transactions, and recoverability of data, respectively. Most often, automated tools are used to schedule jobs, review performance, and help ensure appropriate access authorization. Use of such tools is generally complemented by manual controls performed by management and/or users to review the output of such tools. In addition to the primary function of monitoring the systems, these related areas (use of automated tools, manual review of output, restriction of privileges to modify the tool, etc.) act as complementary controls. For example, if the automated tool used for monitoring is not designed/configured effectively or the ability to modify its configuration is not restricted appropriately, the effectiveness of the review of output is reduced.

The monitoring activities discussed above can directly affect business process controls. For example, batch jobs cause application system programs to be executed. If such programs terminate abnormally (i.e., before the full set of programs has been completely executed), the transaction may not be recorded completely or accurately. Similarly, if certain programs that are necessary for online transactions or batch jobs are not executed, the related items will be inaccurately or incompletely recorded. For example, there might be a batch job that would transfer transaction data from a subledger to the general ledger.

If that program does not transfer all data or does not record it for the correct period near a period end, the completeness or cutoff of those transactions may be impacted.

For the second type of monitoring (also referred to as auditing or logging), tools are generally used by administrators to allow them to take periodic snapshots of the system, identify specific configuration changes or use of "super user" or "emergency" accounts, and assist in resolving any potential control issues. Generally, systems have the ability to log specific events such as unauthorized access attempts or updates to key data. Reports can be periodically generated and timely reviewed by security management and/or system owners. Unauthorized users may access and modify data without detection if violations are not researched timely. Organizations sometimes struggle with the perceived conflict between logging enough information to satisfy audit requirements while not overburdening the system resource constraints by logging mass amounts of data. If correctly designed, the configuration of audit trails should be exception based. For example, logging all purchase orders where there is a large volume of activity may not be useful for reviewing. However, reviewing purchase orders that are of an exceptionally large dollar amount or related to a specific type of procurement (e.g., capital expenditures for assets) would entail a much smaller audit log and be more practical and useful for the reviewer. Similarly, organizations sometimes grant high-level access to IT personnel for emergency purposes. A common mitigating control for the inherent risk in that type of access is to log and review any instances of usage. In theory, the usage should be minimal, and, therefore, the related logging should have a limited system impact.

Integrated Auditing

An integrated audit considers IT, financial, and operational controls as mutually dependent for establishing an effective and efficient internal control environment. When performing an audit, one overall objective is to determine whether controls are effective and efficient in supporting the underlying business processes. As opposed to other types of audits (e.g., financial, operational, compliance), IT audits are unique in that it is sometimes more difficult to tie them directly to an underlying business process. For example, an IT audit may be performed for network security. The underlying business processes that are supported by network security could potentially encompass all business processes that use data transmitted over the network. The implication of this distinction is that findings from an IT audit are not as easily quantifiable when

Chapter 2: What Technology Should Be Audited?

determining their impact in terms of financial, operational, or compliance outcomes.

When performing a financial or operational audit, the objective is to determine whether financial and operational controls are effective and efficient to support the business process. Often the controls within a financial, operational, or compliance audit rely on supporting IT controls. For example, a three-way match may be configured within an accounting application to accurately match purchase orders, invoices, and receipts. When performing a financial audit, the reviewer may validate that the configuration is in compliance with corporate guidance. However, the successful implementation of that control is contingent on a sound IT environment. If the underlying database is not secure, it might be possible to modify that setting without detection for a period of time. If the auditor determined that the underlying database security was weak and this parameter could have been modified, but not detected, how do you assess the risk that this action occurred? How do you quantify the outcome? For these reasons, within an integrated audit, all perspectives need to be considered because IT, financial, and operational issues can impact the achievement of management's objectives of safeguarding information system assets and ensuring the reliability and integrity of information.

The IT portion of an integrated audit includes the applications, servers, and network configurations that support the business process. For example, the IT, financial, and operational auditors collaboratively consider the following as they relate to the business process being examined:

- The business and information processing risks and controls are understood and agreed upon by the business owners, IT delivery and support organization, and the integrated audit team.

- Manual and automated feeds, system interfaces, and communications are accurate, timely, and secure.

- Manual and automated transactions are approved timely and accurately processed.

- Information is secure and privacy controls are in compliance with current regulations and industry standards.

- Disaster recovery plans and business continuity plans provide reasonable assurance that both the system and business operations can recover and continue when a system or business interruption occurs.

- Program changes are authorized, tested, approved, and migrated to production as prescribed by the business process owners.

With all IT audits, though perhaps most critical with the integrated audit approach, is the need to understand the IT environment and structure of the audit area. IT environments are often a complex combination of applications, servers, network components, databases, and interfaces spanning multiple areas of the organization. An initial way to visualize and organize this structure is to separate the IT infrastructure, which includes operating systems, databases, and network components, from the application systems (e.g., an accounts receivable system). This organization is depicted in the following graphic:

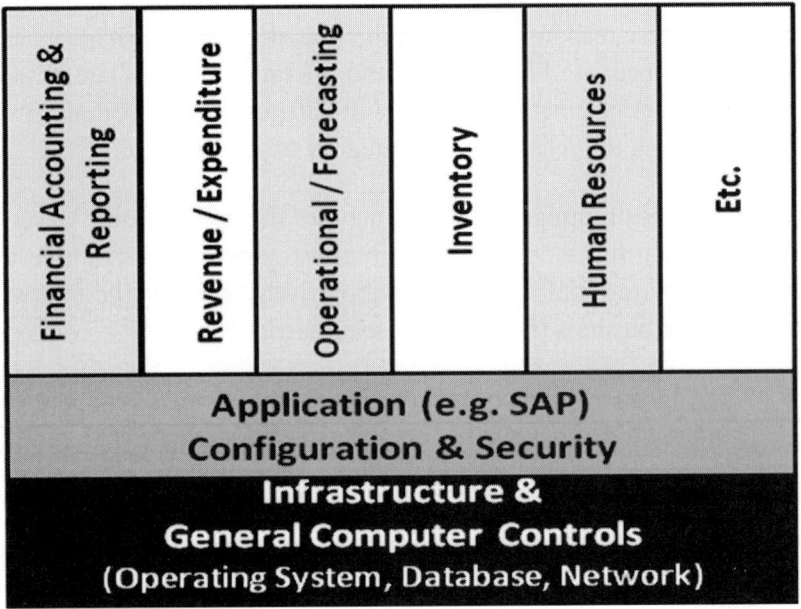

Fig. 1 – Simplified Representation of the Common Elements of an IT Environment

Generally, responsibility for the IT infrastructure will be the function of the IT department, whereas responsibility for the application systems will be within the associated business process or functional area. These responsibilities include ensuring the IT and financial and operational controls are implemented, effective, and efficient.

The business process owner, typically along with the chief information officer (CIO), is ultimately responsible for ensuring the IT and financial and operational controls are implemented, effective, and efficient. Regardless of the overall type of audit being performed, for a comprehensive IT audit, each of the areas outlined in the previous sections (IT strategy through monitoring) should be considered when defining the IT audit scope.

Continuous Auditing

The focus on increased effectiveness and efficiency of assurance, internal auditing, and control has spurred the development of new studies and examination of new ideas concerning continuous auditing, as opposed to more traditional periodic auditing reviews. Several research studies and documents addressing the subject use different definitions of continuous auditing. All of them, however, recognize that a distinctive character of continuous auditing is the short time lapse between the facts to be audited and the collection of evidence and audit reporting. Typically, the collection and evaluation of transactions is automated.

The traditional method of auditing entails performing reviews at defined intervals (e.g., annually, biannually, quarterly, etc.). Due to the periodic nature of reporting during these audits, by the time the findings are published, the process owners may have a much larger set of issues to resolve and management has a more limited amount of time to find timely resolutions to the audit findings. In the context of a financial audit, this can be especially problematic as the audit findings may impact the financial statement audit strategy (e.g., level of substantive testing) and/or the periodic assertions (e.g., Sarbanes-Oxley, OMB A-123, etc.). Conversely, if continuous auditing methods are employed, control exceptions are predefined and relevant parties are notified in real-time. The timely nature of these notifications allows decision makers and process owners not only the ability to correct the initial issue proactively (before being flagged by an auditor), but they can design and implement any additional preventative controls that might be required to avert further instances from occurring in the future.

Another benefit of continuous auditing is for the auditors themselves. When continuous auditing methods are employed, the procedures performed to test the effectiveness of controls can be more efficient. Most audits entail testing a combination of automated controls (e.g., configuration that does not require a sample) and manual controls (e.g., sample-based controls). When continuous auditing is employed, these generally fall into the configuration or "sample of one" category. The auditor can review the auditing configuration and then trace a "sample of one" to validate that it is functioning as intended. Assuming the configuration is designed effectively, there would be no need to test a larger sample of transactions. For example, an organization might implement a control, such as a corporate policy, to limit journal entry approval for particular personnel for defined dollar amounts. Traditionally, an auditor might select a sample of journal entries to determine whether they were approved in accordance with the defined policy. If the control were an automated control (i.e., the configuration of personnel and dollar amounts were defined in the application system), the auditor might inspect the configuration to validate that it conforms with the corporate policy and then review one journal entry to validate that it follows the logic of the configuration. However, there are often instances where management override exists or someone has additional access to function as a backup for the primary user. If a continuous auditing method were employed, such that all instances of noncompliance with the policy were automatically routed to an appropriate reviewer, the auditor would only need to review the automated monitoring configuration and then check the audit trail and/or logs to see that no instances had occurred during the relevant time frame. In theory, continuous auditing can serve as both an effective preventative control and a more efficient audit means.

Some of the drivers of continuous auditing are a need for better monitoring of controls that support the financial reporting objectives, ensuring that real-time transactions also benefit from real-time monitoring, and the use of software to determine that financial, operational, and compliance controls are operating effectively. Another potential benefit of continuous auditing is that it addresses a higher percentage of the population of transactions. As mentioned previously, traditional auditing methods entail selecting a sample of the population and then extrapolating those results to determine the operating effectiveness of the related control. With continuous auditing methods, the process owners and the audit personnel can validate the operating effectiveness for a much larger percentage of the population (in some cases, perhaps, the entire population for a given period) with the same or less effort. This is due to the exception-based nature and real-time monitoring with this approach. Continuous auditing is not a recent development. Many robust applications contain embedded modules with the ability to configure and use continuous monitoring. These would allow an auditor to identify predefined types of events or directly inspect abnormal or suspect conditions and transactions.

Section II
Planning a Technology Audit

IIA Standard 2200 – Engagement Planning
Internal auditors must develop and document a plan for each engagement, including the engagement's objectives, scope, timing, and resource allocations.

2201 – Planning Considerations
In planning the engagement, internal auditors must consider:

- The objectives of the activity being reviewed and the means by which the activity controls its performance;
- The significant risks to the activity, its objectives, resources, and operations and the means by which the potential impact of risk is kept to an acceptable level;
- The adequacy and effectiveness of the activity's risk management and control processes compared to a relevant control framework or model; and
- The opportunities for making significant improvements to the activity's risk management and control processes.

2201.A1 – When planning an engagement for parties outside the organization, internal auditors must establish a written understanding with them about objectives, scope, respective responsibilities, and other expectations, including restrictions on distribution of the results of the engagement and access to engagement records.

2201.C1 – Internal auditors must establish an understanding with consulting engagement clients about objectives, scope, respective responsibilities, and other client expectations. For significant engagements, this understanding must be documented.

2210 – Engagement Objectives
Objectives must be established for each engagement.

2210.A1 – Internal auditors must conduct a preliminary assessment of the risks relevant to the activity under review. Engagement objectives must reflect the results of this assessment.

2210.A2 – Internal auditors must consider the probability of significant errors, fraud, noncompliance, and other exposures when developing the engagement objectives.

2210.A3 – Adequate criteria are needed to evaluate controls. Internal auditors must ascertain the extent to which management has established adequate criteria to determine whether objectives and goals have been accomplished. If adequate, internal auditors must use such criteria in their evaluation. If inadequate, internal auditors must work with management to develop appropriate evaluation criteria.

2210.C1 – Consulting engagement objectives must address governance, risk management, and control processes to the extent agreed upon with the client.

2220 – Engagement Scope

The established scope must be sufficient to satisfy the objectives of the engagement.

2220.A1 – The scope of the engagement must include consideration of relevant systems, records, personnel, and physical properties, including those under the control of third parties.

2220.A2 – If significant consulting opportunities arise during an assurance engagement, a specific written understanding as to the objectives, scope, respective responsibilities, and other expectations should be reached and the results of the consulting engagement communicated in accordance with consulting standards.

2220.C1 – In performing consulting engagements, internal auditors must ensure that the scope of the engagement is sufficient to address the agreed-upon objectives. If internal auditors develop reservations about the scope during the engagement, these reservations must be discussed with the client to determine whether to continue with the engagement.

2230 – Engagement Resource Allocation

Internal auditors must determine appropriate and sufficient resources to achieve engagement objectives based on an evaluation of the nature and complexity of each engagement, time constraints, and available resources.

2240 – Engagement Work Program

Internal auditors must develop and document work programs that achieve the engagement objectives.

> **2240.A1** – Work programs must include the procedures for identifying, analyzing, evaluating, and documenting information during the engagement. The work program must be approved prior to its implementation, and any adjustments approved promptly.

> **2240.C1** – Work programs for consulting engagements may vary in form and content depending upon the nature of the engagement.

CHAPTER 3

RISK ASSESSMENT

To be successful, an organization needs a strategic plan that is based on objectives, risks, and rewards. The primary objectives of any business are to protect the value of its existing assets and create new or future value. To achieve its objective, an organization must identify and assess its risk periodically. Risk assessment is a systematic process for identifying, evaluating, and prioritizing risk. The cornerstone of an effective audit function is performing a comprehensive risk assessment. This ongoing review provides management with an assessment of the key risks that must be controlled or mitigated to enable the organization to achieve its business objectives.

Risk

COSO describes four objectives of an organization that are subject to risk: Strategic, Operations, Reporting, and Compliance. Each of these objectives can be impacted by a number of risks of varying types. One way many of the enterprise risks relevant to technology audits can be classified is under the following categories:

- Governance risk: The risk that decisions or actions taken (or omitted to be taken) by the board and/or management results in significant negative impact on shareholder value and/or the achievement of the organization's goals.

- Strategy risk: The risk of loss resulting from management's inability to develop and implement its long-term plans.

- Operations risk: The risk of loss resulting from inadequate or failed internal processes, people and systems, or external events.

- Infrastructure risk: The risk of loss resulting from inadequate or unsecured IT assets.

- Fraud risk: The risk of financial loss (monetary or otherwise) resulting from fraudulent or illegal acts, typically by employees.

- Reputational risk: The risk that negative publicity will reduce an organization's value or credibility.

- Market(place) risk: The risk posed to an organization by its competitors and the marketplace.

- Regulatory/compliance risk: The risk of loss resulting from a failure to meet legal, regulatory, or compliance requirements.

- External risk: The risk of loss resulting from factors outside the organization's control.

Before understanding a risk assessment and different methodologies governing it, it is imperative to understand what constitutes a risk. Risk may be expressed as an event or action that can adversely affect the organization's ability to achieve its business objective and execute its strategies successfully. Therefore, any event that has a potential for loss of value or sub-optimization of gain for an organization may be viewed as a risk. Per The IIA's *International Standards for the Professional Practice of Internal Auditing* (*Standards*), "Risk may be defined as the possibility of an event occurring that will have an impact on the achievement of objectives." A risk factor is a potential indicator of the existence of, or an increased exposure to, a risk.

Some sample risk factors in an IT environment impacting several of the areas discussed in the previous chapter are:

- New hardware or software acquired/developed is inconsistent with management's intentions (impact on strategy, operations).

- Selection of outsourced IT vendors is inconsistent with policies (impact on sourcing, operations).

- Information systems strategies, plans, and budgets are not aligned with the entity's business and strategic goals (impact on strategy, operations).

- The computer processing environment is not adequately staffed with skilled and experienced personnel (impact on personnel, operations).

- The IT policies and procedures are not documented, approved, or periodically updated (impact on operations).

- Adequate policies have not been established to provide an overall direction and implementation of security (impact on security).

- Physical access restrictions are not duly implemented and administered to confirm that only authorized individuals have the ability to access or use information resources (impact on security).

- Access is not provided on a need to know/need to do basis (impact on security).

- The organization's programs, data, and other information resources are not protected from viruses and intrusions (impact on security).

- Data is not retained in accordance with laws, regulations, customer agreements, and organizational policy to enable retrieval when needed (impact on operations).

- Nonexistence of business continuity and disaster recovery plans (impact on business continuity).

- Data is not backed up to confirm availability of information if the need arises (impact on operations, business continuity).

Risk Assessment Process

Risk assessment is a common first step in a risk management process. Risk assessment is the determination of quantitative or qualitative value of risk related to a concrete situation and a recognized threat. In other words, it is a process for risk identification, evaluation, and prioritization of the organization's key business risks.

To determine an acceptable level of risk, an organization must first understand its risk appetite — the degree to which the organization elects to accept risks without spending resources to mitigate them, or is willing to take on risks that will potentially create new value to the organization (e.g., mergers and acquisitions [M&A] transactions). The risk appetite is subjective in nature and varies from one organization to another. However, it is critical because such an understanding will drive the organization's strategic alternatives in the risk assessment process.

A formal risk assessment process identifies threats and vulnerabilities and is sufficiently broad-based to encompass key internal and external factors. Risk assessment enables the organization to identify assets as well as the risks to those assets, estimate the likelihood of technology failures, and identify appropriate controls for protecting assets and resources. Management evaluates the results of the risk assessment process to prioritize solutions for potential problems, taking into account the severity of likely ramifications and the expense of implementing cost-effective and reasonable safeguards or controls.

IT risk assessment is not a stand-alone process, but an integral part of an organization's overall risk assessment process. While it is often convenient and necessary to identify and assess risks unique to the IT environment, the impact of those IT-specific risks must be evaluated in the context of overall business risks as well.

An important factor to keep in mind is that the risk assessment process (as well as most audits) is itself subject to risk. For example, sampling risk can affect the outcome of the risk assessment process. Sampling risk is the risk that the items or areas being measured do not fully or accurately represent the universe of items to be evaluated. If some, but not all, employees are asked to respond to a survey as part of a risk assessment, the act of selecting a subset of the employee population results in exposure to sampling risk.

There are two components of sampling risk: alpha risk and beta risk. Alpha risk (also known as a Type I error or false positive) is the risk that a significant error or exception does not exist but is identified due to characteristics of the sample selected. A large number of security risks might be identified in a risk survey, but if only the IT security department is surveyed, items that are not truly a significant risk to the business could be falsely included. Beta risk (also known as a Type II error or false negative) is the risk that a significant error or exception is missed or not considered, typically because it was not contained in the sample selected. If no risks to HR are identified, but no one from the HR department participates in the survey, there is an increased risk that areas relevant to the HR department will be overlooked in the risk assessment process.

Chapter 3: Risk Assessment

Objectives of IT Risk Assessment

The objectives of IT risk assessment include aligning with an organization's objectives, risks, and controls. An IT risk assessment enables the organization to better strategically manage risk and (among other benefits):

- Increase system and data reliability.
- Deliver high-quality information quickly and reliably.
- Increase satisfaction of internal and external customers.
- Reduce system complexity and the efforts of maintenance.
- Increase productivity.
- Reduce regulatory costs while remaining compliant.
- Initiate sustainable process improvements across the enterprise.

As per ISACA's IT Audit and Assurance Guideline G13 "Use of Risk Assessment in Audit Planning" section 2.2.2, "The IS auditor should consider each of the following types of risk to determine their overall level:

- Inherent risk.
- Control risk.
- Detection risk."

Inherent Risk (G13 – Section 2.3)

Inherent risk is the susceptibility of an audit area to err in a way that could be material, individually or in combination with other errors, assuming that there were no related internal controls. For example, the inherent risk associated with operating system security is ordinarily high because changes to, or even disclosure of, data or programs through operating system security weaknesses could result in false management information or competitive disadvantage. By contrast, the inherent risk associated with security for a stand-alone PC, when an appropriate analysis demonstrates it is not used for business-critical purposes, is ordinarily low.

Inherent risk for most IT audit areas is ordinarily high because the potential effects of errors usually span several business systems and many users. In assessing the inherent risk, the IT auditor should consider both pervasive and detailed IT controls.

Control Risk (G13 – Section 2.4)

Control risk is the risk that an error that could occur in an audit area and could be material, individually or in combination with other errors, will not be prevented or detected and corrected on a timely basis by the internal control system. For example, the control risk associated with manual reviews of computer logs can be high because activities requiring investigation are often missed, owing to the volume of logged information. The control risk associated with computerized data validation procedures is ordinarily low because the processes are consistently applied.

The IS auditor should assess the control risk as high unless relevant internal controls are:

- Identified.
- Evaluated as effective.
- Tested and proved to be operating appropriately.

Detection Risk (G13 – Section 2.5)

Detection risk is the risk that the IS auditor's substantive procedures will not detect an error that could be material, individually or in combination with other errors. For example, the detection risk associated with identifying breaches of security in an application system is ordinarily high when logs for the whole period of the audit are not available at the time of the audit. The detection risk associated with identifying a lack of disaster recovery plans is ordinarily low because existence is verified easily.

In determining the level of substantive testing required, IS auditors should consider:

- The assessment of inherent risk.
- The conclusion reached on control risk following compliance testing.

The higher the assessment of inherent and control risk, the more audit evidence IT auditors should normally obtain from the performance of substantive audit procedures.[1]

---

[1]"Source: *IT Standards, Guidelines, and Tools and Techniques for Audit and Assurance and Control Professionals.* ©2000 ISACA. All rights reserved. Used by permission."

Risk Assessment and Measurement

There are various risk assessment and measurement techniques available to an IT auditor. They range from simple classification of high, medium, and low to more complex and scientific calculations. An IT auditor should consider the level of complexity and details commensurate with the nature and size of the organization being audited before deciding upon any specific methodology.

Irrespective of the methodology being selected and used, an IT auditor should include an analysis of the risks to the enterprise resulting from the loss of controls supporting system availability, data integrity, and business information confidentiality. All risk assessment methodologies rely on subjective judgments at some point in the process (e.g., classification of risks into high, medium, and low or determining the severity of the impact as minor, moderate, or catastrophic). It is important that the IT auditor identify the subjective decisions required to be used in a particular methodology and consider whether these judgments can be made and validated with an adequate level of accuracy.

According to Section 2.1.4 of ISACA's G13, when deciding upon the most appropriate risk assessment methodology, IT auditors should consider:

- The nature of information required to be collected. Some systems use financial effects as the only measure, which may not be appropriate for IT audits.

- The cost of application and other licenses required to use the methodology.

- The extent to which the information is readily available.

- The cost of obtaining additional information before reliable output can be obtained, including the time required to be invested in the collection of this information.

- The opinions of others using this methodology and their views of how well it has assisted them in improving the efficiency and/or effectiveness of their audits.

- The willingness of management to accept the methodology as the means of determining the type and level of audit work carried out.

Risk Assessment Overview

A typical risk assessment process involves:

- Understanding an organization's business, including strategies and objectives.

- Developing a preliminary understanding of key businesses risks and processes, and aligning them to the organization's strategies and objectives.

- Creating a customized risk universe containing risks faced by the organization.

- Determination of current monitoring activities outside of internal auditing.

- Understanding the effectiveness of entity-level controls.

- Scoping the risk assessment by obtaining input from all stakeholders.

- Assessing, prioritizing, and validating key business risks with the key stakeholders.

- Reporting the results of risk assessment and using those results to develop the audit plan.

Plotting risk factors: Upon assessment of risks, the results can be visually represented by scatter plotting them on a chart. One chart (MARCI) used for plotting the risk factors has four quadrants to categorize risk response actions: Mitigate (M), Assurance (A), Redeploy (R), and Cumulative Impact (CI). A MARCI chart depicts impact, vulnerability, and relative mitigated value rankings of the plotted risks. These can be ranked as high, medium, or low. The chart provides management with a point-in-time assessment of the impact of the significant risks on the organization's value and its vulnerability to these risks. This map assists the organization in the development of the audit plan and should be periodically updated to accurately depict the organization's exposure toward any untoward incident.

Chapter 3: Risk Assessment

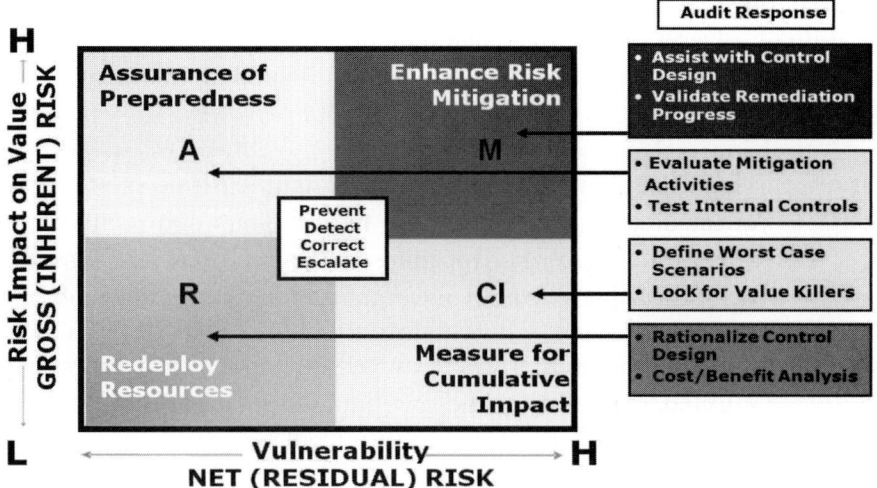

MARCI Chart Axis Definition

The MARCI chart format can be used to show relative relationships between a variety of factors, and is frequently used for multiple purposes. It is important to understand what is being shown and the meanings of the categories for each axis. Many of the terms used have similar or overlapping meanings and can cause confusion if not clearly defined. Two commonly used factors are Impact and Vulnerability, though Impact versus Likelihood, Likelihood versus Vulnerability, and Inherent Risk versus Residual Risk are also commonly seen. Users should agree on what is being defined on each axis for their organization and when the values are calculated.

For example, if risk is measured before mitigating controls are considered, then Vulnerability more likely would be used to refer to the exposure surface of the organization to the risk being measured; while if a risk is measured after mitigating controls are considered, then Vulnerability can be taken to mean the amount of risk to which the organization remains exposed or vulnerable, also sometimes called Residual Risk. To clearly communicate the meaning and implications presented by a MARCI chart, the auditor should clearly define the axes as part of the risk assessment process. For example, the following definitions for Impact and Vulnerability, if included in a risk assessment report containing a MARCI chart, would greatly help a reader to identify what the chart is attempting to show.

Impact: Impact (also called Gross or Inherent Risk) is an estimate of the severity of adverse effects, the magnitude of a loss, or the potential opportunity cost should a risk be realized. Impact is measured for all the relevant risk factors such as Financial Impact, Reputation Impact, Regulatory Impact, etc.

- High: Scenarios where an organization's cash flows are seriously affected, serious diminution in market share and reputation with adverse publicity, or happening of the risk event will significantly deter the achievement of the organization's key business objectives.

- Medium: Scenarios where an organization's cash flows may be affected, market share and/or reputation will be affected in the short term, or happening of the risk event will have some adverse effect on the achievement of the organization's business objectives.

- Low: Scenarios where a negative impact on an organization's cash flows will be absorbed under normal operating conditions or happening of the risk event will have very little or no impact on the achievement of the organization's business objectives and minimal impact on the organization's reputation and/or goodwill.

Vulnerability: Vulnerability (also called Residual Risk) is the extent to which the functional area may be exposed or unprotected in relation to various risk factors after existing controls have been taken into account.

- High: Controls minimally reduce the functional area's exposure to an adverse impact. Controls are primarily either detective or nonexistent.

- Medium: Controls moderately reduce the functional area's exposure to an adverse impact. Controls are primarily detective.

- Low: Controls currently produce the desired result to significantly reduce the functional area's exposure to an adverse impact. Controls are primarily preventative and believed by management to be operating effectively.

Technology Audit Initiatives by Quadrant

- **Mitigate** — Management strategies to reduce or minimize the impact of, or the vulnerability to, a risk, or both.

Chapter 3: Risk Assessment

- **Assure** — Increase the level of confidence that risk exposures are within the organization's risk appetite.

- **Redeploy Resources** — Determine whether risk management resources are better deployed elsewhere.

- **Cumulative Impact** — Investigate further to determine the aggregate impact of a number of small impacting risks.

Risks that have both high impact on the value and high vulnerability, which fall in the (M) quadrant, should be given a high priority and the remediation actions tracked at the executive and program level. For risks that are deemed to be of high impact but low vulnerability due to existing controls or mitigation measures, the organization should confirm that the measurement of vulnerability is realistic and the confidence in preparedness is justified. These risks fall in the (A) quadrant. Risks that have low impact and low vulnerability should be tested and monitored under the normal controls environment and efficiencies identified so that resources dedicated to low-impact, low-vulnerability risk can be redeployed. These risks fall in the (R) quadrant. Risks that have low impact but high vulnerability should be examined independently, but also measured for their frequency and cumulative impact on the organization's objectives; the likelihood that multiple low-impact, high-vulnerability risks occur simultaneously also should be determined. These risks fall in the (CI) quadrant.

OCTAVE®

With the growth of information systems, the confidentiality, integrity, and availability of information plays a vital role in an organization's mission. Organizations should not form protection strategies for their information systems by focusing solely on infrastructure weaknesses and fail to establish or overlook the effects of risk on their most important information assets. When the IT function is solely responsible for an IT risk assessment, it can lead to a gap between the organization's operational requirements and information technology requirements. Often, the IT staff members alone do not have the necessary understanding of the organization's mission or business-related needs. It is not clear whether important information is being adequately protected or significant resources are protecting relatively unimportant information. This is a situation that arises when the operational or business units of the organization and the IT department are not communicating effectively, and the organization might be unknowingly assuming a high level of risk with respect to protecting its information assets.

The Operationally Critical Threat, Asset, and Vulnerability Evaluation (OCTAVE) approach, developed by the Software Engineering Institute (SEI) and available from the Computer Emergency Response Team (CERT), defines the essential components of a comprehensive, systematic, context-driven, and self-directed information security risk evaluation. There are also several alternative approaches that are similar to or based on the OCTAVE methodology. Under the OCTAVE method, the operational or business units and the IT department work together to address the information security needs of the organization. An organization can make information-protection decisions based on risks to the confidentiality, integrity, and availability of critical information technology assets by following the OCTAVE method or a similar approach. The OCTAVE approach is embodied in a set of criteria that define the essential elements of an asset-driven information security risk evaluation.

There are multiple methods consistent with the OCTAVE criteria. For example, the approach would be implemented differently in a very large organization as opposed to a very small one. Presently, the following three methods have been developed, consistent with the OCTAVE criteria:

- OCTAVE method, which forms the basis for the OCTAVE body of knowledge.
- OCTAVE-S, for smaller organizations.
- OCTAVE-Allegro, a streamlined approach for information security assessment and assurance.

The OCTAVE method developed by SEI uses a three-phase approach to examine organizational and technological issues to assemble a comprehensive picture of the information security needs of an organization. The phases are described as:

- **Phase 1: Build Asset-based Threat Profiles** — This is an organizational evaluation. Key areas of expertise within the organization are examined to elicit the knowledge about critical information assets, the threats to those assets, the security requirements of the assets, what the organization is currently doing to protect these information assets (current protection strategy practices), and weaknesses in organizational policies and practice (organizational vulnerabilities).

- **Phase 2: Identify Infrastructure Vulnerabilities** — This is an evaluation of the information infrastructure. The key operational components of the IT infrastructure are examined for weaknesses (technology vulnerabilities) that can lead to unauthorized action.

- **Phase 3: Develop Security Strategy and Plans** — Risks are analyzed in this phase. The information generated from the organizational and information infrastructure evaluations (Phases 1 and 2) is analyzed to identify risks to the organization and evaluate the risks based on their impact to the organization's mission. In addition, an organization protection strategy and risk mitigation plans for the highest priority risks are developed.

Each phase of the OCTAVE method contains two or more processes. Each process is made up of activities. The following list highlights the phases and processes of OCTAVE:

- Phase 1: Build Asset-based Threat Profiles
  - Process 1: Identify Senior Management Knowledge
  - Process 2: Identify Operational Area Management Knowledge
  - Process 3: Identify Staff Knowledge
  - Process 4: Create Threat Profiles
- Phase 2: Identify Infrastructure Vulnerabilities
  - Process 5: Identify Key Components
  - Process 6: Evaluate Selected Components
- Phase 3: Develop Security Strategy and Plans
  - Process 7: Conduct Risk Analysis
  - Process 8: Develop Protection Strategy

Following are some of the important aspects of the OCTAVE method:

Self-direction

The OCTAVE method is self-directed. A small, interdisciplinary team of the organization's personnel (called the analysis team) manages the process and analyzes all information. Thus, the organization's personnel are actively involved in the decision-making process.

Analysis Team

The OCTAVE method requires an analysis team to conduct the evaluation and analyze the information. The analysis team is an interdisciplinary team comprising representatives from both the mission-related and information technology areas of the organization. Typically, the analysis team contains a core membership of about three to five people, depending on the size of the overall organization and the scope of the evaluation.

Workshop-based Approach

The OCTAVE method uses a workshop-based approach for gathering information and making decisions. In Phase 1, key areas of expertise within the organization are examined in facilitated workshops (also called knowledge elicitation workshops). The analysis team facilitates these workshops. Participants in the workshops are from multiple organizational levels. The knowledge elicitation workshops are important for identifying what is really happening in the organization with respect to information security. The outputs for Phase I through the workshops include: list of critical assets, security requirements for critical assets, threats to critical assets, current security practices, and current organizational vulnerabilities.

Catalogs of Information

The OCTAVE method relies upon the following major catalogs of information:

- Catalog of practices — a collection of good strategic and operational security practices.

- Threat profile — the range of major sources of threats that an organization must consider.

- Catalog of vulnerabilities — a collection of vulnerabilities based on platform and application.

An organization that is conducting the OCTAVE method evaluates itself against the above catalogs of information. During Phase 1, the organization uses the catalog of practices as a measure of what it is currently doing well with respect to security (its current protection strategy practices) as well as what it is not doing well (its organizational vulnerabilities). The analysis team also uses the catalog of practices when it creates the protection strategy for the organization during Phase 3.

The OCTAVE method allows an organization to make information protection decisions based on risks to the confidentiality, integrity, and availability of critical IT assets. It also enables business units and IT departments to work together to address the information security needs of the organization.

The Role of Management Sponsorship in the Risk Assessment Process

Management's role in developing an internal risk model that drives subsequent audit planning and testing activities should never be underestimated. Management's commitment and ongoing support is critical to help ensure participation by all necessary participants in internal risk modeling through the risk assessment process. To secure their commitment, the team entrusted with the responsibility of risk assessment and modeling holds an initial meeting with the executives and management to describe the process and its benefit to the organization. Keeping management posted with updates helps in sustaining their interest levels.

Use of Risk Assessment in Audit Planning

Risk assessment in audit planning helps an organization identify risks that can prevent it from obtaining its objective and develop a risk-based audit plan focused on high-risk areas. As per ISACA's IS auditing guidelines G13, "Use of Risk Assessment in Audit Planning," IS auditors should use the selected risk assessment techniques when developing the overall audit plan and planning specific audits. Risk assessment, in combination with other audit techniques, should be considered when making planning decisions such as:

- The nature, extent, and timing of audit procedures.
- The areas or business functions to be audited.
- The amount of time and resources to be allocated to an audit.

A comprehensive risk assessment provides a basis for the development of an IT audit plan that is risk-focused and flexible enough to meet the organization's ever-changing business environment. A year-long IT audit plan may not be an effective way to manage the dynamic needs of the organization. On the contrary, it should be viewed as a living document that is aligned with the business activities and supports management efforts to implement organizational strategies successfully. An audit plan that fails to keep pace with the changes renders the organization vulnerable to significant business risks. Key steps in developing a risk-focused internal audit plan include:

- Mapping the key business risks to auditable units.

- Developing an audit plan that addresses auditable entities with highest risk, disregarding the skill-sets availability.

- Assigning resources with the skill sets necessary to participate in the audits.

- Validating the audit plan with management and the audit committee.

- Revisiting the audit plan as well as updating the risk assessment, as a result of a change to the organization's business environment.

CHAPTER 4

SCOPING

A major challenge faced by both auditors and the management of organizations is to define an effective and efficient scope for the technology audit. The auditors need to understand the organization's technology environment; the applications and computer operations that are part of the technology infrastructure; how technology applications and operations are managed; and how technology applications and operations link back to the organization.

On completing an inventory of technology infrastructure components, the auditors will gain an understanding of the technology infrastructure's vulnerabilities. As defined in *GTAG 1: Information Technology Controls,* "The complete inventory of the organization's IT hardware, software, network, and data components forms the foundation for assessing the vulnerabilities within the IT infrastructures that may impact internal controls." For example, applications and networks connected to the Internet are exposed to threats that do not exist for self-contained applications and networks.

Once an adequate understanding of the technology environment has been achieved, the audit team can perform the risk assessment and identify the scope. While defining the scope, there are a few organizational factors that should be considered, such as the organization's industry, turnover or revenue size, type, the complexity of organizational processes, and geographical location of operations. Two factors — components and role of the technology environment — have a direct impact on the risk assessment and in determining what is included in the audit scope within the technology environment. For example:

- Identifying the technologies used to perform regular business functions.
- Nature of technology environment — simple or complex.
- Nature of technology environment — centralized or decentralized.
- Extent of customization of business applications.

- Determining the extent to which the technology maintenance activities are outsourced.
- Extent of changes to the technology environment every year.
- Any planned application/infrastructure changes for the current year.

These technology factors, among others, are some of the components that auditors must understand to adequately assess risks relative to the organization and the creation of the periodical or special purpose audit plan. In addition to the factors described above, the auditors should use an approach that ascertains the impact and likelihood of risk occurrence, which should link back to the business and also define the high, medium, and low risk areas through other means like quantitative and qualitative analysis. Some of these concepts and tools were discussed in the previous chapter.

Technology is in a continuous state of innovation and change. Due to such continuous changes, the auditor's efforts to identify and understand the impact of risks may be affected. The following steps can help the technology auditors:

- Identify the new technologies that may impact the organization by performing independent annual technology risk assessments.
- Understand the technology department's yearly short-term plan and analyze how the plan initiatives impact technology risk assessment.
- Initiate technology audit scoping by first reviewing its risk assessment component.
- Make changes to the technology audit universe while closely monitoring the organization's technology risk profile and adopt audit procedures as it evolves.

There are several IT governance frameworks that can help audit teams develop the most appropriate risk assessment approach for their organization. These frameworks can help auditors identify where the risks reside in the environment and provide guidance on how to manage these risks. Some of the commonly accepted IT governance frameworks include *Control Objectives for Information and Related Technology* (*COBIT*), IT Infrastructure Library (ITIL), and the International Organization for Standardization's (ISO's) 27000 Standard series. Mapping business processes, inventorying and understanding the technology environment, and performing a companywide risk assessment will enable auditors to determine what needs to be audited and how often. Detailed guidance on some commonly accepted frameworks is provided in the next section.

Knowledge of the Organization

The work of the technology auditors should be planned before the audit begins in a manner appropriate for meeting the audit objectives. As a part of the planning process, they should understand the organization and its processes. This will help them determine the significance of the technology resources being reviewed as they relate to the objectives of the organization and understand the organization's operations and its technology requirements.

The extent of the knowledge required by the technology auditors will be determined by the nature of the organization and the level of detail at which the audit work is being performed. They may require specialized knowledge when dealing with unusual or complex operations. If the audit scope involves a wide range of information system functions, they would need extensive knowledge of the organization and its processes as compared to the audit where only limited functions are scoped. For example, a review with the scope of evaluating control over an organization's change management process would ordinarily require a more thorough understanding of the organization than a review with the objective of testing controls over a specific program library system.

The technology auditors should understand the types of events, transactions, and practices that can have a significant effect on the audited organization, function, process, or data that is included in the scope for the audit. Knowledge of the organization should include the business, financial, and inherent risks facing the organization as well as conditions in the organization's marketplace. It should also include the extent to which the organization relies on outsourcing to meet its objectives. The technology auditors should use this information in identifying potential problems, formulating the objectives and scope of the work, performing the work, and considering the actions of management.

Top-down, Risk-based Approach

One of the key responsibilities (and also a complex task) of an auditor is to create the organization's audit scope. There have been various approaches to defining the scope of an audit engagement. For example, the SEC, the Public Company Accounting Oversight Board (PCAOB), and The IIA's GAIT methodology have recommended a top-down and risk-based approach to defining Sarbanes-Oxley Section 404 scope and related key controls. Although the above mentioned guidance focuses on Section 404 assessment and scoping, the principles of the guidance also can be applied to the identification of controls for other assessment purposes (e.g., as part of an assessment of controls for regulatory compliance).

As IIA Standard 2010: Planning explains, the CAE must establish risk-based plans at least annually to determine the priorities of the internal audit activity and define the scope, which, in turn, should be consistent with the organization's goals and strategies. This has been documented by The IIA Research Foundation's (IIARF's) Common Body of Knowledge 2006 study, which found that nearly all CAEs interviewed plan their audit activities at least annually, including 36.4 percent who update their audit plan multiple times per year (Figure 1). Additional guidance also has been published by organizations, including ISACA, relative to the assessment of controls within technology organizations.

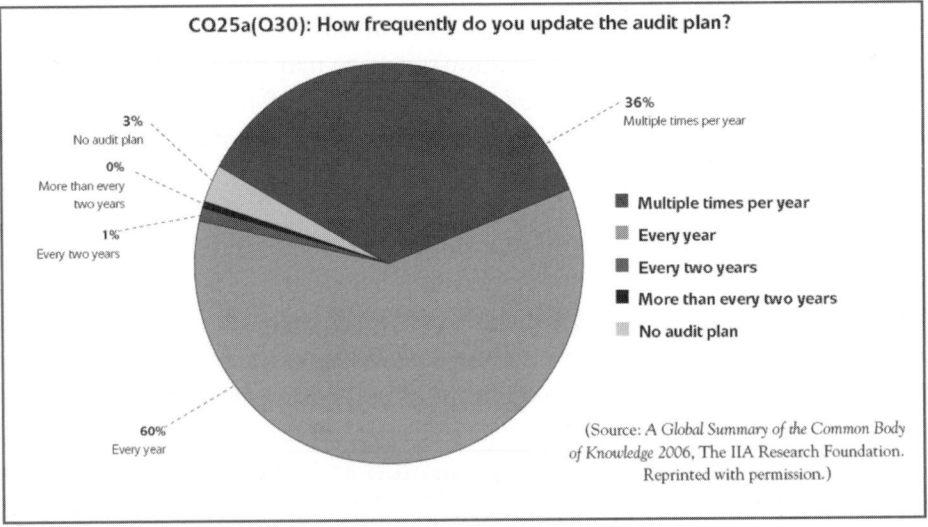

Figure 1. Frequency of audit plan updates

The assessment of entity controls should be performed early in the process, as suggested by both the SEC and PCAOB. The information obtained from such assessment of risks and controls at the entity level can be considered in assessing risks and related controls at lower levels, such as those in general technology control processes. The information obtained from the entity-level controls assessment work should be considered when defining the scope of the technology audit, as it may affect the assessment of the likelihood of certain general technology control process failures (for example, in the case of the control related to staffing the organization with appropriately qualified and trained personnel). If there are issues in this area in technology, such that inexperienced individuals are building applications, it might indicate a higher risk that the application controls are less than adequate.

The top-down, risk-based approach identifies the key business objectives and processes, major applications that support such key business processes, the infrastructure needed for the business applications identified, the organization's service support model for technology, and the role of common supporting technologies such as network appliances. By using these technical components, along with an understanding of service support processes and system implementation projects, auditors will be able to create a comprehensive inventory of the technical environment. This inventory, in turn, forms the basis for assessing the vulnerabilities that may impact internal controls. Once auditors have a clear picture of the organization's technology environment, they will be able to perform the risk assessment. The previous chapter discusses some methodologies and tools used for risk assessment.

The information and analysis results gained by understanding the organization, inventorying the technology environment, and assessing risks helps to formalize the audit scope and plan. The objective of the audit plan is to determine the scope of the audit so that the auditors can focus on providing management with objective information to manage the organization's risks and control environment.

During this exercise, an important perspective to understand is that technology only exists to support and advance the organization's objectives and is a risk to the organization if its failure results in the inability to achieve a business objective. Hence, it is important to first understand the organization's objectives, strategies, business model, and the role that technology has in supporting the business. This can be achieved by identifying the risks found in the technologies used and how each risk might prevent the organization from meeting a business objective. Doing this would result in more meaningful and useful assessments for management. Also, the auditors need to be more familiar with the organization's business model. Because each organization has a unique set of business goals and objectives, business models help auditors identify the products or services the organization provides, its market base, supply channels, manufacturing and product generation processes, and delivery mechanisms. By gaining this fundamental knowledge, auditors will be able to understand unique business risks and how technology supports existing business models and mitigates the organization's overall risk profile. Technology auditors should also coordinate with business and/or financial auditors to understand the business risks and the technology components that are critical to the advancement of the organization.

Once the auditors become familiar with the organization's entity-level strategic objectives, they will be able to identify the key processes that are critical to the objectives' success. While doing so, they need to understand how each business process differs within different departments, operating units, support functions, and key organizationwide projects, as well as how the process relates and links to entity objectives. Project processes are unique, but equally vital, in ensuring initiatives that add value to the organization are managed and commercialized appropriately. A process is considered key if its failure prevents the organization from fully achieving the strategic objective to which it is tied.

Once key processes are identified, auditors need to delineate the important applications and essential technology infrastructure (e.g., database, operating system, network, and physical environment) supporting these applications. Underlying these applications and technology infrastructure are supporting technology processes, such as systems development life cycles, change management, operations, and security activities. The applications may require periodic assessments based on their significance to various factors such as financial reporting activities, regulatory compliance, or operational requirements. Examining the operating environment this way (i.e., starting from the top of the organization) will help auditors understand and inventory each critical component. They need to fully understand the operating environment and its risks, which require that different technology factors that influence and help categorize organizational risks are comprehensively understood.

Bottom-up, Risk-based Approach

Most organizations use the top-down, risk-based approach. However, a technology audit scope also can be created based on a general technology process risk identified using a bottom-up approach. For example, an auditor might reference an application, database, network item, operating system (OS), or checklist that suggests that a certain risk or technology component is important and question why it has not been included in the technology audit scope. It is doubtful that a risk brought up in this fashion (bottom-up rather than top-down) would represent a likely risk to prevent the organization from fully achieving its strategic objective. Some examples to help understand the issues or technology component that may help identify audit items to be included in the scope are:

- If the issue is router configuration, include the network security or application/database potentially affected in the audit scope.
- If the issue is database administrator privileged access to the data, identify the applications that use that database for inclusion in the audit scope.

Once the application/database/network component is identified, the auditors may include the same or general technology control processes that encompass this technology component into the audit scope.

The bottom-up approach also can help in identifying the audit scope by enhancing a risk matrix, which assists in strategically assessing the level of risk associated with general technology processes. To start, an organization should identify what constitutes a risk factor in the context of its business. The level of risks (high, medium, low) could be defined for each risk factor. For example, one of the common risk factors can be "change management," and the organization may define what constitutes a high level of risk to the organization versus medium- or low-level risk.

For each general technology process or technology component within the organization, a risk rating or priority level is provided and the overall risk is determined. To establish the individual as well as overall ratings, discussion with key stakeholders should be undertaken and professional judgment applied. Because not all risks or issues have equal impact, additional weights are assigned to risk factors, as required. For example, data security may have a higher weight compared to change management for a certain IT general process.

Regulatory-based Approach

There are many laws and regulations such as Sarbanes-Oxley, the Basel II Accord, European Union (EU) regulations, and numerous others across the globe that mandate the use of internal controls and risk management practices and the privacy of personally identifiable information. There are other regulations that mandate the protection of information in specific industries, like the Gramm-Leach-Bliley Act (GLBA), the Payment Card Industry Data Security Standard (PCI DSS) (which regulates customer information in the credit card industry), and the Health Insurance Portability and Accountability Act (HIPAA) in the health-care industry for the safeguarding of personal medical information. Most of these regulations do not address technology controls directly; however, they imply the need for an adequately controlled technology environment.

There are regulatory audits that would have limited areas of an organization's processes or components in scope for a compliance review that might include both technology and non-technology elements. In these cases, the scope of the audit is confined to the few areas under review and defined by the regulation in question. These audits are either measured directly against the requirements defined in the regulation, such as HIPAA, or measured against some framework, such as COBIT or ISO.

There are other audits that include regulatory audit and compliance as one of the subjects of the audit scope and universe. The scope for such audits is driven by the regulations in question but can also include a risk-based approach. In both of these assignments, the auditors must determine whether the organization has rigorous processes in place and whether they are operating effectively to help ensure compliance.

There is another type of audit where the scope is defined by other bylaws or requirements by virtue of relations with other organizations or business relationships. Such audits are limited scope reviews that are more narrowly focused than a full scope audit. One such example is an audit against a service-level agreement (SLA), a specific framework, or both.

One of the critical risks associated with a regulatory scoped audit is compliance risk. This risk arises from violation of, or nonconformance with, laws, rules, regulations, prescribed practices, or ethical standards. This risk also arises in situations where laws or rules governing the business or industry are vague, confusing, or newly implemented. This risk exposes the organization to fines, penalties, payment of damages, and cancellation of contracts. It can lead to diminished reputation, reduced business value, limited business opportunities, lessened expansion potential, and lack of contract enforceability.

Other Approaches

Technology audit scoping also can be influenced by various other factors, including personal preference, the audit function's operating budget, staffing considerations, or where the auditors think they can add the most value. However, in doing such scoping, the management/auditor should try to scope the work in a manner that provides the most efficient and effective audit and reduces or limits redundancy and duplication of effort.

One method is to look at the audit area as one single process, begin from the business transactional starting point, and drop it where the business process interfaces with one of the technology stack layers or components. The audit is continued from the point where the technology provides the output to the business process and conducted until the logical end of the process. In such an audit, the scope does not include the technology portion of the process, although a complete end-to-end process is audited. Similarly, one of the other methods of scoping a technology audit is to pick up the transactions within the technology component and audit through the passage of various layers or stacks, but not audit the process before or after the transaction enters/leaves the technology component. These scenarios emphasize that there are various approaches to scoping an audit and none is necessarily incorrect or incomplete. The scope also could be determined by the requests from stakeholders such as the board of directors, the audit committee, senior managers, business or IT managers, other relationships (shareholders, vendors, contractual parties, customers, and auditors), or various regulatory bodies.

There is no single right way to scope a technology audit, but there are incorrect or inappropriate ways to do the scoping. Examples include incorrect sizing of the audit universe due to incomplete knowledge of the environment, or basing a plan solely on staffing capabilities. Also, the audit scope should be divided so as to reasonably size the audits and allocate the audit resources appropriately. When doing so, auditors should understand that defining an overly narrow or broad audit scope might hamper audit efforts. This is because a certain amount of overhead is required for each audit engagement, including administrative efforts for audit scoping, planning, management reviews, sign-offs of completed work, and reporting and communicating results. If the audit universe and plan contains numerous audits with smaller scope, for example, auditors could spend as much time administrating the audits as performing them. Similarly, if the audit scope is defined broadly, audits could run for an extended period of time, be disruptive to the audited organization, or be reviewed insufficiently. Depending on the organization's culture, excessively broad scope definitions might even result in an unplanned increase in scope (also known as scope creep).

CHAPTER 5

FRAMEWORKS AND STANDARDS

A successful organization is built on strong frameworks that provide industry-recognized leading practices. The use of various IT frameworks enables an organization to implement practices that can help IT processes deliver the information that the business needs to achieve its objectives. An IT control framework can be described as a set of commonly recognized practices for information technology management. Such a framework provides managers, IT auditors, and users with a set of generally accepted measures, indicators, processes, and commonly recognized practices to help them maximize the benefits derived through the use of IT. It also helps in developing appropriate IT governance and control in an organization.

As IT has become more important, organizations are looking for recognized practices they can use to implement IT policies and procedures. IT professionals, organizations, and government agencies have come together to share information and develop recognized practices for information technology. The industry-leading IT frameworks can be categorized as:

- Commonly recognized IT frameworks or practices.
- Technical frameworks or practices.
- Marketplace practices administered by third parties.

Specific versus Generic Standards

Many organizations planning to implement an IT framework are often in a dilemma regarding the selection of an appropriate framework. The answer, of course, is that it depends on what an organization wants to accomplish. For instance, if the choice has to be made between COBIT and ISO/IEC 27002:2005, then the organization should understand the difference between these frameworks. As COBIT is an internationally recognized standard for control of governance of IT, ISO/IEC 27002:2005 is equally recognized and established in the field of information security management. These two standards do not compete against each other — they are mutually complementary. COBIT by its nature is broader, whereas ISO/IEC 27002:2005 tends to be deeper in the area of information security. As such, the COBIT framework focuses more on general information technology controls. Thus it has a broader coverage of general information technology topics, but does not have as many detailed information security requirements as the ISO framework. If an organization addresses all of the security controls within ISO/IEC27002:2005, it will cover a large part of the COBIT framework in the process — especially section DS5 "Ensure Systems Security." However, COBIT covers a much larger set of issues related to IT governance, and is typically used as part of an overall corporate governance framework.

Following are some of the benefits of using a control framework:

Structured: A control framework provides an excellent structure that organizations can follow. Furthermore, the structure helps everyone communicate because they share a common understanding of what is expected.

Best Practices: The frameworks are developed over a period of time and assessed by hundreds of people and organizations all over the world. The cumulative years of experience reflected in the models cannot be matched by a single organization's efforts.

Knowledge Sharing: By following a framework, people can share ideas between organizations and benefit from user groups, websites, magazines, books, and so on. Organization-specific ad hoc approaches do not have this luxury.

Auditable: Use of a standard framework helps the auditors to effectively assess controls. By this, it also implies that the auditors themselves may take advantage of frameworks, as opposed to using ad hoc auditing practices.

Time and Effort: Use of an already developed, documented, and tested framework helps the organization by saving time and effort.

Adopt and Adapt: Use of a framework allows quick setup of the process within the organization, with room to adapt the framework to suit organizational demands.

As per the "Information Security Harmonization – Classification of Global Guidance" document issued by ISACA, following is a list of the most common and generally practiced security guidance:

Chapter 5: Frameworks and Standards

- **BS 7799 Part 2:2002 Information Security Management Systems — Specification with Guidance for Use:** Specifies the requirements for establishing, implementing, operating, monitoring, reviewing, maintaining, and improving a documented information security management system [this guidance is now implemented as the ISO 27000 series of standards].

- **Control Objectives for Information and related Technology (COBIT):** Represents a collection of documents that can be classified as generally accepted framework and standards for IT governance, security, control, and assurance. Published by the IT Governance Institute.

- **Systems Security Engineering — Capability Maturity Model (SSE-CMM) Model description Document 3.0:** Provides the concepts and application of a model to improve and assess security engineering capability.

- **Generally Accepted Information Security Principles (GAISP):** A collection of security principles that has been defined and produced by members of the various organizations involved.

- **The Information Security Forum's (ISF's) Standard of Good Practice for Information Security:** Presents a collection of information security principles and practices.

- **ISO/IEC 13335 Information Technology — Guidelines for the Management of IT Security:** Provides information security management technical guidance subdivided into five parts. Published by the International Organization for Standardization and the International Electrotechnical Commission.

- **ISO/TR 13569: 1997 Banking and Related Financial Services — Information Security Guidelines:** Offers a grouping of security concepts and suggested control objectives and solutions for financial sector organizations. Released by the International Organization for Standardization.

- **ISO/IEC 15408:1999 Security Techniques — Evaluation Criteria for IT Security:** Provides a reference to evaluate and certify the security of IT products and systems. Based on the Common Criteria for

Information Technology Security Evaluation 2.0 (CC). ISO/IEC 15408:1999.

- **ISO/IEC 17799:2000 Information Technology — Code of Practice for Information Security Management:** Presents a collection of information security practices.

- **The IT Infrastructure Library's (ITIL's) Security Management:** Describes how IT security management processes link into other IT infrastructure management processes.

- **NIST 800-12 An Introduction to Computer Security — The NIST Handbook:** Describes the common requirements for managing and implementing a computer security program and offers guidance on the types of controls that are required. Released by the U.S. National Institute of Standards and Technology (NIST).

- **NIST 800-14 Generally Accepted Principles and Practices for Securing Information Technology Systems:** Presents a collection of principles and practices to establish and maintain system security.

- **NIST 800-18 Guide for Developing Security Plans for Information Technology Systems:** Provides a format and guidance for developing a system security plan.

- **NIST 800-53 Recommended Security Controls for Federal Information Systems:** Provides a set of baseline security controls.

- **Operationally Critical Threat, Asset, and Vulnerability Evaluation (OCTAVE):** Presents a set of principles, attributes, and outputs for risk assessment.

- **Organization for Economic Co-operation and Development (OECD) Guidelines for the Security of Information Systems and Networks:** Provides a set of nine information security principles aimed at fostering a "culture of security."

- **Open Group's Manager's Guide to Information Security:** Provides general guidance for IT managers on acquiring secure IT products and systems.

Chapter 5: Frameworks and Standards

In spite of numerous security standards, frameworks, and practice, no single framework of IT governance can fit the needs or objectives of every organization. Each business must look at its own challenges, goals, and objectives and evaluate the available frameworks to see which features of each best help to meet those goals. Each of the frameworks brings its own strengths to the current business environment. For instance, ITIL is strong on IT service management, ISO is strong on security, whereas COBIT's strength is most pronounced in the area of controls and metrics.

It is not within the scope or intention of the authors of this book to provide guidance on all of the pros and cons of these and other commonly recognized IT frameworks. Much information is available in the public domain on the Internet.

The following discussion is not based on any particular IT framework or commonly recognized practices. It is management's or the auditors' responsibility to determine the components of these and other frameworks that best serve the organization. It is also important to keep in mind that none of these frameworks is a one-size-fits-all tool. In fact, these frameworks can be used in combination simultaneously by organizations to manage and improve their IT functions as well as by auditors to develop testing procedures.

As with any commonly recognized IT framework or practice, management and auditors should proceed with caution when using these frameworks and practices as a basis for their activities. They must understand and apply the framework's concepts and guidance in their correct context. For example, COBIT has been developed and refined over the last decade with the assistance of professionals, organizations, and different industries from around the globe. As a result, it tends to have the look and feel of a framework that might work appropriately in a large organization with a sizable technology function, but may be challenging to work with in medium-sized and small organizations. Additionally, the management and audit team should realize that simply because the technology function does not follow or conform to the COBIT framework, it does not mean that the function and its processes or data are not controlled or managed correctly. At a minimum, management and auditors can use COBIT as a helpful guide during the technology risk assessment and audit process. In a best-case scenario, the management and audit team should integrate the use of COBIT under the umbrella of risk and control-related frameworks and guidance, as well as to help the technology function with the implementation of part or all of the components within the framework.

Commonly Recognized IT Frameworks or Practices

Commonly recognized IT frameworks are used by organizations to develop and monitor IT programs or processes. These frameworks provide management with the required toolset for developing organizational policies and procedures. They also provide the auditors with recognized industry practices that can be used for the development of technology audit testing objectives and/or procedures. Some of the industry-leading commonly recognized IT practices are discussed below in more detail (in alphabetical order).

COBIT

COBIT is a set of commonly recognized practices (framework) for IT management created by ISACA and the IT Governance Institute (ITGI) in 1992. COBIT provides managers, auditors, and IT users with a set of generally accepted measures, indicators, processes, and commonly recognized practices to help them maximize the benefits derived through the use of IT and develop appropriate IT governance and control in an organization.

COBIT includes a range of support items and tools, including performance measurement items, a list of critical success factors, and maturity models for benchmarking and comparison. COBIT provides good practices across a domain and process framework and presents activities in a manageable and logical structure. Its good practices represent the consensus of experts. They are strongly focused more on control and less on execution. These practices help optimize IT-enabled investments, help ensure service delivery, and provide a measure against which to judge when things do go wrong. For IT to be successful in delivering against business requirements, management should put an internal control system or framework in place. The COBIT control framework contributes to these needs by:

- Making a link to the business requirements.
- Organizing IT activities into a generally accepted process model.
- Identifying the major IT resources to be leveraged.
- Defining the management control objectives to be considered.

The business orientation of COBIT consists of linking business goals to IT goals, providing metrics and maturity models to measure their achievement, and identifying the associated responsibilities of business and IT process owners. The process focus of COBIT is illustrated by a process model that subdivides IT into four domains and 34 processes in line with the responsibility areas of plan, build, run, and monitor, providing an end-to-end view of IT. The 34 COBIT processes, grouped into four domains, are:

- Plan and Organize.
- Acquire and Implement.
- Deliver and Support.
- Monitor and Evaluate.

Each process has a numeric level of maturity from 0–5 (0 is nonexistent and 5 is optimized). This scale can be used for a number of key evaluations, such as the level of maturity a process currently resides within an organization, what level of maturity the processes should be, what level is considered best practice, and what level the best of your competitors/other organizations have achieved. Recently, ISACA released Val IT, which correlates the COBIT processes to senior management processes required to get good value from IT investments. ISACA has also released Risk IT, a framework complimenting COBIT to help enterprises identify, govern, and manage risk.

COBIT was released and used primarily by the technology community and has become the internationally accepted framework for IT governance and control. ISO/IEC 17799:2005 (the Code of Practice for Information Security Management; now the ISO 27000 series of standards and discussed in detail later in this section) is also an international standard and an industry-leading framework/practice for implementing security management. The two standards do not compete with each other and in fact complement one another. COBIT typically covers a wider area while ISO/IEC 17799 is deeply focused in the area of security.

Public companies that are subject to Sarbanes-Oxley are encouraged to adopt COBIT and/or COSO's *Internal Control – Integrated Framework*. In choosing which of the control frameworks to implement, the SEC has suggested the COSO framework as a suitable model, and many organizations supplement it with COBIT.

COBIT is closely related to the COSO control framework and provides additional guidance related to IT. COBIT approaches IT control by looking at information broadly — not just financial information — that is needed to support business requirements and the associated technology resources and processes. The two frameworks have different audiences but complement one another well.

The benefits of implementing COBIT as a governance framework over IT include:

- Better alignment of IT processes based on a business focus.
- A view of what IT does that is understandable to management.
- Unambiguous ownership and responsibilities, based on process orientation.
- Acceptability with third parties and regulators.
- Shared understanding among all stakeholders, based on a common language.
- Fulfillment of the COSO requirements for the IT control environment.

COSO

In 1992 COSO published *Internal Control – Integrated Framework*. As directed by Section 404 of Sarbanes-Oxley, the SEC adopted related rules for public companies. The SEC indicated that the COSO framework may be used as an evaluation framework for purposes of management's annual internal control evaluation and disclosure requirements.

Internal Control – Integrated Framework states that internal control is a process, established by an entity's board of directors, management, and other personnel, designed to provide reasonable assurance regarding the achievement of stated objectives. COSO's control objectives focus on the effectiveness and efficiency of operations, reliable financial reporting, and compliance with laws and regulations. COSO is useful for organizational management at large and applies to internal controls as a whole, while COBIT is primarily useful for IT management, users, and auditors. The COSO framework contains five components intended to address internal control:

- Control Environment.
- Risk Assessment.
- Control Activities.
- Information and Communication.
- Monitoring.

COBIT as a framework is specifically focused on IT controls, which are more narrowly focused than COSO. Due to this difference, auditors should not expect a one-to-one relationship between the five COSO control components and the four COBIT objective domains. Many organizations use both of these frameworks as a basis for internal controls.

Chapter 5: Frameworks and Standards

COSO subsequently released guidance for enterprise risk management in 2004 based on the material developed in the initial *Internal Control – Integrated Framework* model, which expands on the concept and use of controls throughout an organization, including the IT function. The ERM framework contains eight components:

- Internal Environment.
- Objective Setting.
- Event Identification.
- Risk Assessment.
- Risk Response.
- Control Activities.
- Information and Communication.
- Monitoring.

ISO 17799/27000 Series

ISO 17799/27000 was commonly called ISO 17799 as a result of the popularity it gained at the time. The ISO 27000 series of standards is an expanded and updated version that is an internationally recognized generic information security standard published by ISO and the International Electrotechnical Commission (IEC). This standard is also known as *Information technology – Security techniques – Code of practice for information security management*. It consists of a comprehensive set of controls comprised of the commonly recognized practices in information security. It is intended to serve as a single reference point for identifying a range of controls needed for most situations where information systems are used in industry and commerce. It can be used by any organization that needs to establish a comprehensive information security management program or improve its current information security practices.

The ISO standard establishes guidelines and general principles for initiating, implementing, maintaining, and improving information security management in an organization. The objectives outlined provide general guidance on the commonly accepted goals of information security management. It contains commonly recognized practices of control objectives and controls in:

- Risk assessment.
- Security policy.
- Organization of information security.
- Asset management.

69

- Human resources security.
- Physical and environmental security.
- Communications and operations management.
- Access control.
- Information systems acquisition, development and maintenance.
- Information security incident management.
- Business continuity management.
- Compliance.

The control objectives and controls in ISO are intended to be implemented to meet the requirements identified by a risk assessment. It is intended as a common basis and practical guideline for developing organizational security standards and effective security management practices, and to help build confidence in inter-organizational activities.

ISO 17799/27000 is a comprehensive information security standard that provides organizations with benefits such as:

- An internationally recognized and structured methodology.
- A defined process to evaluate, implement, maintain, and manage information security.
- A set of tailored policies, standards, procedures, and guidelines.
- Certification that allows organizations to demonstrate their own and evaluate their trading partners' information security status.
- Certification that shows due diligence.

IT Infrastructure Library (ITIL)

The ITIL is a set of concepts and policies for managing IT infrastructure, development, and operations. ITIL is one of the most widely accepted approaches to IT service management. It provides a cohesive set of industry-leading practices, drawn from the public and private sectors internationally.

ITIL is a consistent and comprehensive documentation of industry-leading practice for IT service management. Used by hundreds of organizations around the world, an entire ITIL philosophy has grown up around the guidance contained within the ITIL books and the supporting professional qualification scheme. ITIL consists of a series of books that provide guidance on the provision of quality IT services and the accommodation and environmental facilities needed to support IT. ITIL has been developed in recognition of organizations' growing dependency on IT and embodies commonly recognized practices for IT service management. The ethos behind the development of ITIL is the recognition that organizations are becoming increasingly dependent on IT to satisfy their corporate aims and meet their business needs. This leads to an increased requirement for high-quality IT services.

ITIL provides a systematic and professional approach to the management of IT service provision. Adopting its guidance offers users a range of advantages. ITIL:

- Provides a single, definable, repeatable, and scalable documented framework for commonly recognized IT practices that flows across the IT organization.
- Identifies roles and responsibilities for IT service management.
- Supports reducing IT costs and justifies the cost of IT quality.
- Supports the ability of IT to measure and improve internal performance and service provisioning.
- Defines IT in terms of services rather than systems.
- Supports improvement of user productivity.
- Improves communication and information flows between IT and organization business departments.
- Provides a framework for IT to support regulatory challenges.
- Improves the ability of IT to adjust as business opportunities and challenges are presented.
- Improves the relationship of IT with the business and builds trust.

ITIL addresses in depth the various aspects of service management, but it does not address enterprise architecture in similar depth. Many of the weaknesses in the implementation of ITIL do not necessarily come about because of flaws in the design or implementation of the service management aspects of the business, but rather the wider architectural framework in which the business is situated. Because the primary focus of ITIL is on service management, it has limited utility in managing poorly designed enterprise architectures, or the process to feed back into the design of the enterprise architecture.

Software Capability Maturity Model

The Capability Maturity Model (CMM) for software, developed by Carnegie Mellon's Software Engineering Institute and various industry and government affiliates in the early 1990s, is a process maturity model or framework that helps organizations improve their software life cycle processes. The model is particularly adept at enabling organizations to prevent excessive project schedule delays and cost overruns by providing the appropriate infrastructure and support necessary to help projects avoid these issues.

Standard of Good Practice (SoGP)

The Standard of Good Practice (SoGP) is a detailed documentation of identified good practices in information security. The standard, first released in 1996, is revised every two or three years by the Information Security Forum (ISF), an international association of organizations in financial services, manufacturing, consumer products, telecommunications, government, and other areas. SoGP is available free of charge for noncommercial use from the ISF, whereas other ISF reports and tools are generally available only to member organizations.

SoGP is developed from research and actual practices and incidents experienced by member organizations, ISF's research, comprehensive benchmarking program, analysis of other standards and prevailing practices, and direct feedback from and active involvement of ISF members. Its regular and relatively frequent update cycle (typically every two years) allows it to keep current with technological developments and emerging threats. The standard is used as the default governing document for information security behavior by many organizations, by itself or in conjunction with other standards such as ISO/IEC 27002 or COBIT.

SoGP was updated most recently in February 2007 to include a new addition focusing on user environments. It also includes expanded sections on application security, risk assessment, and sections addressing regulatory compliance and evolving security issues arising out of the ISF's recognized practices research and recommendations.

Technical Frameworks or Practices

Technical frameworks, or practices, are published by information technology practitioners and vendors. These practices can come in the form of checklists or as case studies that can be used with some minor customization to reflect the organization's specific requirement. The checklists tend to be very technical in nature, in some cases actually recommending the specific system settings. Such checklists or case studies are not meant to be complied with completely as the settings or items are only ideal settings and recommended based on leading practices and commonly recognized practices. However, not all items or

Chapter 5: Frameworks and Standards

settings can be complied with due to the varied business requirements within an organization.

Significant material is available in the public domain relating to industry-leading practices contributed by IT practitioners, in addition to the materials supplied by vendors. Some of the technical frameworks or practices used by organizations currently include the National Institute of Standards and Technology (NIST), the Center for Internet Security (CIS) benchmarks, and the SysAdmin, Audit, Network, Security (SANS) Institute's top 20 list. Some of these are discussed in detail below in alphabetical order. These can be helpful guidance as they often reflect real-world scenarios. Practitioners that are out in the field actually trying the recommendations on these checklists typically prepare these frameworks. The sources, reliability, and relevance of these frameworks/practices should be considered before using them in the business environment. All checklists should be modified before using as required to reflect the organization's requirements.

Audit Programs and Internal Control Questionnaires

Audit programs and internal control questionnaires are tools used by auditors to assess and evaluate the design and operating efficiency of various processes and controls within an organization as part of an audit. Audit programs and internal control questionnaires are designed based on aspects such as the industry to which the client belongs, the control environment existing within the client organization, the policies and procedures, previous audit findings, and regulatory environment in which the client operates. Various regulatory and academic bodies publish audit programs and internal control questionnaires that could be used by the auditors during their audit after suitable customization. Following are some examples of audit programs and internal control questionnaires published by The IIA in its GTAG series, ISACA, and the Federal Financial Institutions Examination Council (FFIEC):

- IIA GTAG Programs
  - IT Change Management
  - Data Processing/Application
  - Identity and Access Management
  - IT Projects

- ISACA Published Audit Programs*
  - E-commerce Security

- - o Unix Operating System
    - o Change Control
    - o Incident Handling

- FFIEC Published Audit Programs
  - o Business Continuity Planning
  - o Electronic Banking
  - o Information Security
  - o Retail Payments Systems

*Note: ISACA audit programs can only be obtained by ISACA members with the appropriate level of access.

Center for Internet Security (CIS)

The CIS is a not-for-profit organization that helps enterprises reduce the risk of business and e-commerce disruptions resulting from inadequate technical security controls, and provides enterprises with resources for measuring information security status and making rational security investment decisions. CIS members develop and encourage the widespread use of security configuration benchmarks through a global consensus process involving participants from the public and private sectors. The practical CIS benchmarks support available high-level standards that deal with the "Why, Who, When, and Where" aspects of IT security by detailing "How" to secure an ever-widening array of workstations, servers, network devices, and software applications in terms of technology specific controls. CIS scoring tools analyze and report system compliance with the technical control settings in the benchmarks.

The center strives to reduce the frequency of failures and attacks and the losses that arise from them. Its mission is to help organizations around the world effectively manage the organizational risks related to information security by providing them with methods and tools to improve, measure, monitor, and compare the security status of their own Internet-connected systems and appliances, plus those of their business partners. The center is not tied to any proprietary product or service. It manages a consensus process whereby members articulate security threats that concern them, followed by prioritization and development of benchmarks and accreditation methodologies to reduce the threats of concern to members. The consensus process is already in use and has proved viable in creating widely adopted Internet security practices. By enabling joint action to reduce risks, the center strives to represent the shared interests of:

- Network and IT users — the individuals, organizations, universities, government agencies, and not-for-profits that depend on secure and reliable cyber systems.

- Auditors and security consultants who need explicit technical benchmarks and accredited auditing tools to evaluate network reliability and help ensure that they are accurately measuring the right things.

- Network security administrators, firewall administrators, and systems security specialists whose job is to help ensure the security, privacy, integrity, and availability of information assets under their custodial care.

- Business-to-business e-commerce exchanges, network operators, and others who have a direct stake in minimizing risk exposure of IT users to network disruptions and cybercrime.

- Insurance providers — the people whose business is to quantify the costs of risks and enable organizations to insure against resulting damage.

- Investors and consumers who need a way to identify businesses and networks that have taken appropriate steps to help ensure their security and reliability.

National Institute of Standards and Technology (NIST)

The NIST is a nonregulatory federal agency within the U.S. Department of Commerce. NIST's Computer Security Division provides standards, guidelines, and other resources for information security professionals and other interested parties. It issues standards and guidance for various legal requirements, including:

- E-Government Act of 2002.
- Federal Information Security Management Act of 2002 (FISMA).
- Health Insurance Portability and Accountability Act (HIPAA).

- Homeland Security Presidential Directive-7 (HSPD-7).
- Homeland Security Presidential Directive-12 (HSPD-12).
- OMB Circular A–11: Preparation, Submission, and Execution of the Budget.
- OMB Circular A-130: Management of Federal Information Resources, Appendix III: Security of Federal Automated Information Resources.

NIST information security documents include Federal Information Processing Standards (FIPS), the Special Publication (SP) 800 series, Information Technology Laboratory (ITL) Bulletins, and NIST Interagency Reports (NISTIR).

- The FIPS publication series relates to standards and guidelines adopted and promulgated under the provisions of FISMA.

- The Special Publication 800-series reports on ITL's research, guidelines, and outreach efforts in information system security and its collaborative activities with industry, government, and academic organizations.

- Each ITL Bulletin presents an in-depth discussion of a single topic of significant interest to the information systems community. They are issued as needed.

- The NIST Interagency Report series may report results of projects of transitory or limited interest. They also may include interim or final reports on work performed by NIST for outside sponsors (both government and nongovernment).

Adopting the standards and guidance from NIST provides the following benefits:

- Using NIST guides provides assistance in complying with FISMA.

- NIST provides specification for minimum security requirements for federal information and information systems using a standardized, risk-based approach.

Chapter 5: Frameworks and Standards

- NIST defines minimum information security requirements (management, operational, and technical security controls) for information and information systems in each such category.

- Identify methods for assessing the effectiveness of security requirements.

- Help bring the security planning process up to date with key standards and guidelines developed by NIST.

- Provide assistance to agencies and the private sector by conducting ongoing, substantial reimbursable and non-reimbursable assistance support, including many outreach efforts such as the Federal Information Systems Security Educators' Association (FISSEA), the Federal Computer Security Program Managers' Forum (FCSM Forum), the Small Business Corner, and the Program Review for Information Security Management Assistance (PRISMA).

- Evaluate security policies and technologies from the private sector and national security systems for potential federal agency use by hosting a growing repository of federal agency security practices, public/private security practices, and security configuration checklists for IT products. Also, in conjunction with the government of Canada's Communications Security Establishment, NIST's Computer Security Division (CSD) leads the Cryptographic Module Validation Program (CMVP). The Common Criteria Evaluation and Validation Scheme (CCEVS) and CMVP facilitate security testing of IT products usable by the federal government.

National Security Agency (NSA)

The U.S. National Security Agency/Central Security Service (NSA/CSS) is the cryptologic organization for the United States. The NSA protects U.S national security systems and produces foreign signals intelligence information. In addition, NSA, through its Information Assurance (IA) division, provides various guides on information assurance security solutions that help users by providing a deep understanding of risks, vulnerabilities, mitigations, and threats. The following lists some of the guidance provided by NSA:

- **Media Destruction Guidance:** The guidance helps meet specific NSA performance requirements for sanitizing, destroying, or disposing of media containing sensitive or classified information.

- **Security Configuration Guides:** NSA develops and distributes configuration guidance for a wide variety of software, both open source and proprietary. It provides the best possible security options for the most widely used products.

- **Standards Profiles:** NSA, tasked by the Defense Information Systems Agency (DISA), completed a series of standards profiles. These documents identify the mandatory features for the industry standard, based on the architectural context, and address secure interoperability with enterprise services offered by DISA. DISA has included the profiles in the acquisition documentation for the Net-Centric Enterprise Services (NCES) Program and requires that potential vendors comply with these standards profiles. NSA adopted these standards to encourage and enable enterprisewide interoperability, information exchange, and accessibility across networks, as well as to extend information to business partners, stakeholders, and the public.

- **System-level Information Assurance Guidance:** NSA provides system-level guidance to Information Systems Security Engineering (ISSE) for a significant number of U.S. system development efforts. To assist system developers who face similar challenges, the guidance is published as generalized guidance. Although beneficial, this generalized guidance is not a substitute for the sound ISSE activity that should be an integral part of all system development efforts.

Marketplace Practices Administered by Third Parties

The third type of commonly recognized IT framework or practices is marketplace practices. These practices are independent standards that signify a certain level of security. They are similar to certifications in that organizations must meet certain criteria to become certified. This has become very prevalent in the marketplace, where consumers want to see that organizations that conduct business online, for example, have met certain standards related to privacy and security. In the market, these standards go a long way in providing credibility related to privacy and security for organizations with an online presence. Some examples include:

- **GlobalSign:** It is one of the credible and known certificate authority (CA) and Secure Sockets Layer (SSL) providers. It issues trusted digital certificates delivering its public trust from a trusted public root. These trusted roots are recognized by all operating systems, major Web browsers, Web servers, e-mail clients, Internet applications, and devices that require SSL certificates. As a WebTrust accredited public certificate authority, GlobalSign offers publicly trusted SSL, including EV SSL Certificates, S/MIME, and Code Signing Certificates for use on all platforms, including mobile devices. These digital certificate solutions allow many customers to conduct secure online transactions and data transfer, distribute tamper-proof code, and bind identities to client certificates for e-mail security and remote two-factor authentication.

- **VeriSign:** It is one of the trusted providers of internet infrastructure services for the networked world. It provides SSL and identity and authentication services, among others, which allow organizations and consumers to engage in trusted communications and commerce.

Section III
Performing a Technology Audit

IIA Standard 2300 – Performing the Engagement
Internal auditors must identify, analyze, evaluate, and document sufficient information to achieve the engagement's objectives.

2310 – Identifying Information
Internal auditors must identify sufficient, reliable, relevant, and useful information to achieve the engagement's objectives.

Interpretation:
Sufficient information is factual, adequate, and convincing so that a prudent, informed person would reach the same conclusions as the auditor. Reliable information is the best attainable information through the use of appropriate engagement techniques. Relevant information supports engagement observations and recommendations and is consistent with the objectives for the engagement. Useful information helps the organization meet its goals.

2320 – Analysis and Evaluation
Internal auditors must base conclusions and engagement results on appropriate analyses and evaluations.

2330 – Documenting Information
Internal auditors must document relevant information to support the conclusions and engagement results.

2330.A1 – The chief audit executive must control access to engagement records. The chief audit executive must obtain the approval of senior management and/or legal counsel prior to releasing such records to external parties, as appropriate.

2330.A2 – The chief audit executive must develop retention requirements for engagement records, regardless of the medium in which each record is stored. These retention requirements must be consistent with the organization's guidelines and any pertinent regulatory or other requirements.

2330.C1 – The chief audit executive must develop policies governing the custody and retention of consulting engagement records, as well as their release to internal and external parties. These policies must be consistent with the organization's guidelines and any pertinent regulatory or other requirements.

2340 – Engagement Supervision
Engagements must be properly supervised to ensure objectives are achieved, quality is assured, and staff is developed.

Interpretation:
The extent of supervision required will depend on the proficiency and experience of internal auditors and the complexity of the engagement. The chief audit executive has overall responsibility for supervising the engagement, whether performed by or for the internal audit activity, but may designate appropriately experienced members of the internal audit activity to perform the review. Appropriate evidence of supervision is documented and retained.

Performing an IT Audit

There are as many ways to structure and approach a technology audit as there are technologies to audit. The specific approach, while important, is not as important as understanding the bigger picture of what the audit is trying to accomplish. A thorough understanding of the purpose of the audit allows for flexibility of the audit approach and an ability to adapt to the changes and variety that occur with every technology environment on a continual basis. The audit plan that was performed in a preceding year will be less likely to be useful as more and more time passes. In fact, when compared to an audit plan for a business process, a technology plan is more generic to begin with and ages more quickly as well. The implication of this is that a strong understanding of the technology environment and how it operates will allow you to more effectively revise and update audit work programs.

To provide a manageable understanding of the technology environment within any organization, and from audit to audit, a consistent model should be employed to quantify and represent the entirety of an organization's IT assets and processes. This allows a consistent approach to planning and prioritizing the annual audit universe and subsequent plan as well as ensuring comprehensive coverage of the risks, controls, processes, and requirements of the technology function is obtained. The degree of granularity used for the model will vary based on need and culture within each organization, from simple and broad to extraordinarily detailed and fine-grained. A business with low risk and simple processes might represent their technology function with a simple 3x4 matrix detailing IT processes and technology platforms as illustrated below.

		Processes		
		Change Management	Operations	Security
Technologies	Applications			
	Databases			
	Operating Systems			
	Network			

This allows them to audit by process (change management across any technology), by technology (all processes impacting a particular platform), or a subset of targeted audits at any intersection of the matrix.

A larger organization with more risk and complexity (or more internal audit resources) might have a more granular list of processes and bucket activities into: Policies and Procedures, User Access and Segregation of Duties, Systems Configurations, Change Management, Controls Over Data, and Monitoring and Reporting. Although more targeted and specific in nature, the combination of identified processes (for example, User Access and Segregation of Duties and Controls Over Data into a larger classification, such as Security) should still end up providing equal coverage of the activities of the technology function. The advantage of this approach is that it can be easily expanded to create either finer detail or greater coverage. For example, a fourth column titled Regulatory Compliance could be created for a regulated entity, or a fourth row titled Mobile Devices could be added if that were a significant area of concern for management. The important thing to keep in mind is that regardless of how many rows and columns you end up deciding are appropriate for a particular organization, the model should be used consistently over time with as little alteration as possible. That means it must be broad enough in setting up the initial classifications to be flexible enough to absorb new processes or technologies without significant modifications to the model. This will allow for consistent planning to occur on a year-by-year basis and a better understanding of the organization's technology environment over time.

Depending on how you structure your approach to a technology audit, the following are some recommended scope and topic considerations you might evaluate or include (in no particular order):

- **Application Systems**
  - Project planning and management
  - Systems design and acquisition
  - Systems development and testing
  - Systems rollout and turnover
  - Change control and maintenance
  - Application administration
  - Application security and configuration
- **Business Continuity Planning**
  - Data backup and recovery
  - Business continuity planning
  - Disaster recovery planning

- **Business Process IT Controls**
  - Masterfile data
  - Transaction processing
  - Application configuration
  - Application security
  - User access and segregation of duties
  - System interfaces
  - Reporting
  - User-managed applications
- **Databases**
  - Database design
  - Database configuration
  - Database administration and monitoring
  - Database change management
- **Hardware Support**
  - Hardware approval and acquisition
  - Hardware implementation and testing
  - Hardware support and maintenance
  - Hardware performance monitoring
  - Hardware disposal
- **IS Operations**
  - Job scheduling
  - Performance monitoring
  - Event management
  - Physical access
  - Environmental controls
- **Information Security**
  - Security policies and standards
  - Data ownership
  - Information security architecture
  - Access management systems
  - Security administration
  - Logical access
  - Security logging and monitoring
- **Information Systems Strategy and Planning**
  - IS strategy
  - IS budgeting
  - IS staffing
  - IS training

- **Network**
  - Network design
  - Network configuration
  - Network administration
  - Network change management
  - Network performance monitoring
- **Operating Systems**
  - Operating system acquisition
  - Operating system configuration
  - Operating system administration
  - Operating system change management
- **Relationships with Outsourced Vendors**
  - Outsourced service provider selection
  - Outsourced service provider contracts
  - Service-level agreements
  - Service-level evaluation and monitoring

As an exercise in understanding the technology environment, try to identify the row and column that would be appropriate for each of the listed areas above based on the matrix pictured previously.

For the purposes of this text we are using the 3x4 model illustrated above; we will present each technology separately and discuss the audit concerns relevant to that technology, broken down into Change Management, Operations, and Security-related buckets. This will allow us to provide an understanding of the concepts related to technology audits without having to get bogged down in the particular details of how one technology differs from another in a specific area, as such differences are too numerous to catalog. For specific guidance on particular technologies or IT activities, The IIA provides a continually growing body of practice guides known as the GTAG series, which is available for electronic download on their website.

When performing a technology audit, the basic expectations for the activity are provided by IIA Performance Standard 2300 (and its associated Practice Advisories), as included at the beginning of this section.

These standards can be supplemented with additional guidance relevant to the particular technology or process being audited, but special care should be taken to help ensure specific guidance developed by an organization itself is considered and followed.

Regardless of the technology or process being audited, there are some aspects to the audit process that remain the same, such as the difference between a manual and an automated test. However, it is important to keep in mind that just because a technology is used in a process or a test does not mean that the process or test is automated. One particular area in which to exercise caution is the reviewing of computer-generated reports. Two things to keep in mind are: the process of reviewing (and possibly reconciling) the report is a manual process even if the report was generated automatically, and if the underlying data from which the report is generated is not verified to be accurate, complete, up to date, and sufficiently precise to provide a valid result before the report is generated and reviewed, the results cannot be trusted to accurately reflect the environment.

Depending on the approach used, a test can be either manual or automated, depending on how it is performed. For example, newer versions of the Microsoft Windows operating system have a tool known as the Security Configuration and Analysis Tool, which can compare all of the configurable security settings of a system against a template of predetermined or desired settings (perhaps proscribed by corporate policy or industry best practice) and the deviations identified in an output report. The same test could be performed by observing each of the system settings and comparing them against the same proscribed criteria, but when done manually, the test is much less efficient. The fact that the use of technology can assist the auditors in the performance of their duties has given rise to Computer Assisted Audit Techniques (CAATs), but they are still responsible for understanding the tests, results, and interpretations that arise from the use of CAATs and should not depend on a tool to provide as useful or insightful an outcome as their own work should.

CHAPTER 6

NETWORKS

Sample Risks	Sample Control Activities
Operations: A network device failure negatively impacts the timely flow of data.	• Critical network devices are deployed in a redundant manner to provide failover capabilities. • Critical network devices are monitored on an ongoing basis to identify potential performance issues before impact.
Security: Unauthorized access to a network device results in disruption of network services or diversion of network traffic.	• Administrative traffic to all network devices requires unique authentication and is encrypted to prevent eavesdropping. • Auditing of administrative activities is enabled and remotely logged for all critical network devices. • An out-of-band network is used for all administrative activities.
Change Management: Network is subject to frequent unplanned outages due to maintenance or administration activities.	• Network changes are documented, tested, and approved before implementation. • Configuration baselines (standards) are documented and used for the deployment of all network devices.

Networks and networking are responsible for the movement of data between various computers and other devices for the purpose of performing computing activities and sharing information. Networks are the "plumbing" that connect the various nodes and endpoints in transaction processing and control the "flow" of information in the IT environment. Networks can interoperate because they conform (to greater or lesser degrees) to a common set of design and operational specifications. There are a plethora of protocols and standards that govern networking, many of which have been issued a Request for Comments (RFC) document, which is released to the public and interested parties for discussion before being adopted as a de facto or "open" standard. An Internet search for specific RFCs will provide detailed technical information on the design and functioning of any aspect of a network being considered for an audit.

Networks have both physical and logical properties and connections. Physical elements of a network include the copper or fiber-optic cable or wireless links between devices as well as routers, switches, firewalls, bridges, modems, and monitoring tools. Logical elements of networks include packaging, routing, addressing, and tracking of data delivery and communication sessions. One of the most basic logical concepts for networking is that of Internet protocol (IP) addresses (IPv4 established in RFC 0791). IP addresses are defined in quad dotted decimal format, which results in unique identifiers for each system such as 192.168.14.218 or 10.27.237.164. Each segment of an IP address is represented in binary (machine language) format by 8 bits (a bit being either a single 0 or 1) and is referred to as an octet. IP addresses are restricted to numbers between 0 and 255 for a total of 256 (2^8) possible values due to memory and processing limitations of computers and so range between 0.0.0.0 and 255.255.255.255. This allows for a total of approximately 4.2 billion (256^4) unique addresses. This limitation is in part addressed by network address translation (RFC 1618) and classless inter-domain routing (RFC 1517 and 4632) for the short-term.[1]

---

[1] In the long term, this limitation and other concerns such as security are being addressed with a new specification known as IPv6 (RFC 2460), which provides for addresses made up of eight groups of four hexadecimal characters (0123:4567:89ab:c def:0123:4567:89ab:cdef), resulting in 2^{128} possible addresses. Many organizations are only now beginning to deploy IPv6 networks in conjunction with their existing IPv4 networks. According to the European Internet numbering authority (RIPE), as of a June 2009 survey, IPv6 accounted for traffic equal to or greater than IPv4 in less than two percent of responding entities. Informal surveys of the Internet namespace in late 2009 indicate less than six percent of entities have (accessible) IPv6 networks.

Because this is a finite number, the IP address space has been divided into public and private address space (RFC 1918). Private addresses are 10.0.0.0-10.255.255.255, 172.16.0.0-172.31.255.255, and 192.168.0.0-192.168.255.255 and are reserved for the internal common shared use among networks not connected to the Internet (i.e., they are considered "non-routable" across public networks). The use of non-routable addresses allows for systems to be connected and disconnected from a network frequently with the assignment of an address being reused each time a new machine is connected. This allows for a limited pool of addresses to service a larger pool of systems (as long as they are not all connected at the same time). Most of the remaining addresses are considered public addresses and are assigned to systems and entities that are connected to the Internet and available at all times. Public addresses are uniquely associated with specific machines and are not reassigned in the manner of private addresses. Companies such as Google, Amazon, IBM, and others can be identified by their IP address. It is common for a company to use a mix of public and private addresses. Public addresses are assigned to resources that are always available, such as the corporate Web server and mail server, and private addresses are assigned on a dynamic basis to internal users as they connect and disconnect their laptops when moving from office to office. Internal resources that must be accessed regularly by many users, such as an ERP application server, typically have a private address that is statically assigned.

The specifications for network communication design, implementation, and functionality are primarily developed by the Institute of Electrical and Electronic Engineers (IEEE), the Internet Engineering Task Force (IETF), the Internet Assigned Numbering Authority (IANA), and various network hardware manufacturers. The specifics for most aspects of networking can be found in IEEE standards and RFCs issued by standards bodies that provide all of the technical information necessary to design, build, and operate network equipment. For example, RFC 1918, issued by the IETF February 1996 and titled "Address Allocation for Private Internets," discusses the reasoning and approach for using private IP address blocks and supersedes two earlier RFCs on the same topic.

Because of the complexity and variety inherent in networking, several models have been postulated to help understand the environment in a simplified form. The two most common are the seven-layer Open Systems Interconnect (OSI) model developed by the ISO as ISO 7498 and the four-layer TCP/IP model developed by the IETF and sometimes called the DoD model after work that was done for the U.S. Department of Defense. The benefits of these models extend beyond the granularity they provide in designing and implementing networks as they really provide a common language and perspective for anyone involved in networking, simplifying communication and classification of equipment, risks, and a consistent understanding of the environment.

The more common OSI model is a logical abstraction of the communication process between two systems, with each layer handling a different aspect of the communication session. This modularity simplifies the development and coding of applications by offloading intersystem code development and the handling of data transmission as a separate process for which an application developer no longer needs to be responsible. The OSI model is typically illustrated as follows:

Layer #	Layer Name	Description	Sample Protocols
7	Application	Works closest to the user providing file transmissions, terminal sessions, message exchanges, etc.	Web browser, Telnet, FTP, DNS, SNMP, Database Software, Print Server Software
6	Presentation	Provides a common means of representing data in a structure that can be appropriately processed by the end system. Also handles data compression and encryption.	ASCII, Unicode, HTML, JPEG, GIF, TIFF
5	Session	Establishes, maintains, and releases communications between computers.	Remote Procedure Call (RPC) NetBIOS Structured Query Language (SQL)
4	Transport	Provides end-to-end data transport services and establishes the logical connection between two communicating computers.	Transmission Control Protocol (TCP) User Datagram Protocol (UDP) Secure Sockets Layer (SSL)

Layer #	Layer Name	Description	Sample Protocols
3	Network	Inserts information into the logical header of each network data transmission packet for routing (logical addressing).	Internet Protocol (IP v4 and IP v6) Internet Control Message Protocol (ICMP) Routing Information Protocol (RIP)
2	Data Link	Changes the data into 1's and 0's based on the OS for the physical layer. Provides physical addressing.	Serial Line Internet Protocol (SLIP) Point-to-Point Protocol (PPP) Fiber Distributed Data Interface (FDDI) Asymmetric Digital Subscriber Line (DSL) Integrated Digital Services Network (ISDN) Media Access Control (MAC)
1	Physical	Converts bits of data into voltage for actual transmission.	Cables (CAT 1-5, Coaxial) Fiber Distributed Data Interface (FDDI) Asymmetric Digital Subscriber Line (DSL) Integrated Digital Services Network (ISDN)

There are two popular mnemonics for remembering the layers of the OSI model: (from layer one to seven) "Please Do Not Throw Sausage Pizza Away" and (from layer seven to one) "All People Seem To Need Data Processing."

Each layer of the network "stack" or portion of the operating system code designed to handle network communications has certain functions that it performs for both inbound and outbound messages. Each layer passes the message on to either the layer below it or above it, depending on whether the message is outbound or inbound. Each layer interacts with its counterpart on the corresponding remote system, that is, any function done by one layer on the outbound machine is processed by the same layer on the inbound machine.

An understanding of the various layers of networking is necessary because there are different risks associated with each layer. Based on the type of device and the layer at which it operates, the auditors' concerns and the tests they perform will vary accordingly. One important consideration to keep in mind is that a compromise or failure at a particular layer affects not only that layer but all higher layers as well. For example, if a network is compromised at layer 3 (the network layer), the layer that handles IP addressing, then all layers above must be considered compromised as well. In this case, any information that is captured in log files that identifies specific IP addresses is suspect, while any data that identifies MAC addresses (layer 2) is still reliable.

The four layer TCP/IP model consists of application or process layer, transport or host-to-host layer, Internet or internetworking layer, and link or network access layer. Although there are fewer layers in this model, all of the functionality defined in the granularity of the more formal OSI model is captured (albeit in a more flexible fashion) and it more closely typifies the actual real-world operation of networks. This model can be illustrated and mapped to the OSI model as follows:

DoD Layer	**DoD Name**	**OSI Layer**	**OSI Name**
4	Application	7 6 5	Application Presentation Session
3	Transport	4	Transport
2	Network	3	Network
1	Link	2 1	Data Link Physical

It is important to note, however, that the two models do not align cleanly and they should not be used interchangeably as they have different underlying assumptions and different precise meanings for the same or similar terminology. Both models can be used simultaneously, however, as many networking professionals are familiar with both — as long as a clear distinction is made as to which model is being referenced and for what purpose.

When data is sent across a network, it is broken up into small pieces called packets, datagrams, or frames depending on the layer that is handling the operation and type of network. The size of the pieces (in terms of bytes) varies based on the type of network. If a large packet traverses a network with a smaller frame size, the original packet is split into smaller packets and sent on its way. Ultimately all of the received packets are reassembled at their destination to recreate the original message. As a message such as a request for a particular Web page is crafted, the following activities occur in relation to each of the seven layers of the OSI model previously introduced:

1. A Web browser (application layer) requests a connection with the remote Web server.
2. The connection is monitored throughout the duration of the transaction (session layer).
3. The connection is established on a logical "port" (a unique numeric value up to 65,535 that is not related to the physical ports found in networking equipment). For example, Web servers operate on "port" 80 (transport layer).
4. The request is sent to the logical IP address of the Web server (network layer).
5. The network hardware matches the logical IP address to the actual physical MAC address of the Web server (Data Link Layer).
6. The signal carrying the request is sent across the wire to the Web server (physical layer).
7. The Web server responds by sending back the HTML code (presentation layer) to be displayed in the browser.

As the request goes through each of the various layers, the network stack adds additional information to the data received from the layer above it. When the transport layer receives the request, it appends the port number and other related information to the packet before handing the (now larger) packet to the networking layer, which appends the IP address (and other required information) before handing the packet to the Data Link Layer, which appends additional management information, and so on. This additional data, which is necessary for the transmission but enlarges the original request, is known as "overhead" and varies with the type of network and traffic. Much of network troubleshooting involves the inspection and interpretation of this management information found in the packet "headers" or information prepended to the actual data to be sent.

The two most common network types are Carrier Sense Multiple Access Collision Detection (CSMA/CD) typified by the Ethernet standard (IEEE 802.3) and token ring (IEEE 802.5). An Ethernet network operates by sharing the available bandwidth among all connected devices simultaneously so that any device that has data to send listens to the wire and, if it determines the line is free, sends its data. This can result in two or more devices sending data at the same time, resulting in a collision and subsequent loss of the data packet. If a system determines a collision has occurred, it (and the other connected systems) wait a random amount of time and attempt the transmission again. The underlying assumption is that eventually the transmission will be completed. This design allows for efficient use of the network as no computer has to wait very long to use the network, resulting in low latency. However, the more systems connected to an Ethernet network the more likely a collision is to occur. This means that an Ethernet network becomes saturated or unable to handle the volume of transmissions with a much lower number of connected systems than a token ring network.

In contrast to the underlying design assumptions of the Ethernet standard, a token ring network is structured to avoid collisions entirely and optimize the reliability of data transmission by allowing only one or a limited number of systems to transmit data at any given time. This is accomplished through the use of a special data packet called a "token" that is passed around the network from one machine to the next. Any machine that has the token is allowed to transmit; all others must wait until the token is released and passed to the next waiting system. In this design model, many more systems can be connected to a network without the confusion and retransmissions necessitated by a collision detection scheme.

The distinction between the two models leads to a key operational aspect of network design and management, which is selecting the appropriate model to meet business needs and then monitoring traffic levels and the number of connected systems to optimize the performance of the network.

The most common devices found in a network are:

- Hubs.
- Switches.
- Routers.
- Bridges.
- Gateways.

Chapter 6: Networks

- Modems.
- Wireless Access Points (WAPs).
- Firewalls.
- Intrusion Detection and Intrusion Prevention Systems (IDS and IPS).
- Network Interface Cards (NICs).
- Workstations.
- Servers.
- Virtual Private Networks (VPN).

To understand how a network functions and the types of risks a network is subject to, it is necessary to understand what each device is intended to do and how it operates.

A hub is the simplest and least expensive of the networking devices and provides a means to interconnect multiple devices to transmit data between systems. It does this through the connection of each device or "node" to a "port" or receptacle on the hub itself. Hubs typically have four or eight ports, and they receive a data transmission from one node and then broadcast the information to all remaining ports, essentially functioning as a multiport repeater. This means that any device connected to a hub can eavesdrop on all data transmitted by every other device connected to the same hub, resulting in a fundamental security risk. Hubs are a "one-to-many" design and operate at the lowest layer of the OSI model, layer 1.

Switches are also used to interconnect multiple devices, but they have some intelligence built into them that allows them to track which devices are connected and what communication sessions are in process between various machines. The switch then limits the transmission of data to only those ports involved in the communication session and does not broadcast or repeat the data across all ports. Because of their additional capabilities, switches are more expensive than hubs. Switches typically operate at layer 2; however, more modern hardware can operate at layer 3 or even layer 4 of the OSI model.

Routers also can be used to interconnect devices, but while hubs and switches are primarily used for connecting endpoints or nodes to a network, routers are most commonly used to connect multiple networks together for the purpose of communicating between different networks and to physically segment large networks into more manageable or secure sub-networks or "subnets." One of the most common uses of a router is to connect a corporate network to the Internet, which is itself simply a massive network of interconnected networks.

97

As its name implies, a router is primarily responsible for determining the path or "route" the data will travel as it moves across a network to its ultimate destination. Routers typically operate at layer 3 of the OSI model, but they also can operate at layer 4.

Both bridges and gateways perform the same function, which is to connect networks with different underlying protocols (e.g., Ethernet and token ring) together; however, bridges typically operate at layer 2 of the OSI model, while gateways can operate at any level and frequently have additional functionality such as firewalling capabilities.

Modems (**mo**dulator-**dem**odulators) are used to convert the digital signal generated by computers into an analog signal so that data can be transmitted over phone lines where the receiving system uses another modem to convert the analog signal back to digital for processing. Modems pose a particular risk as they are frequently left connected to systems even when not in use, providing a potential backdoor for attackers to attempt to enter a network illicitly.

WAPs provide a means for nodes to connect to a network without the need for a physical attachment; however, because the wireless spectrum is a broadcast medium (meaning that all devices in range can see the signal), they operate much like hubs and have many of the same associated risks in addition to those uniquely related to broadcast communications because they do not have a physical transmission medium that can be secured. Many techniques have been implemented to address these vulnerabilities, such as cloaking of signals, encryption of transmissions, restrictions on allowed connections, screening of antennas, etc. which add to the complexity and overhead of both administering a wireless network and auditing a wireless network.

Firewalls are specialized access control devices that provide a chokepoint between networks and allow for the inspection and potential rejection of both incoming (ingress) and outgoing (egress) traffic. Firewalls operate based on sets of rules configured by network technicians and can function at almost any layer of the OSI model. The simplest firewalls are packet inspection firewalls that look at the header information for each packet that passes through them and make decisions based on the source and destination information. This is typically done at layer 3 of the OSI model. Because this is a labor intensive process with a large impact on performance, stateful packet inspection firewalls were developed to provide faster throughput and more robust security. They do this by observing the state of a communication session and, once an authorized session is established, ignoring all remaining packets that are part of the session. Stateful packet inspection firewalls operate at layer 4 of the OSI model. There are also application proxy firewalls that act as intermediaries in the data flow. They intercept traffic on behalf of the user based on an understanding of the application in use and initiate their own session with the destination machine without letting the original packets flow through the firewall. This has the added benefit of hiding the true identity of the requestor and masking all of the systems behind the firewall.

Intrusion Detection Systems and Intrusion Prevention Systems are designed to perform similar security functions with slightly different response actions. Both types of devices monitor the flow of network traffic looking for specific threats or unusual traffic patterns, but an IDS simply provides a notification of an identified threat to a human operator or log file, while an IPS has an active response and is capable of sending information to a firewall to reconfigure the rule set and block the suspect traffic.

Network interface cards (NICs) are hardware input/output components installed in computer systems to allow them to connect to a network. The network stack is the portion of the operating system responsible for managing the operation of the NIC.

Workstations are the individual terminals or personal computers connected to the network. Workstations are not usually included as a component of a network audit.

The term "server" has multiple meanings, depending on the context is which it is used. Server can refer to software, hardware, or both. Frequently, servers are computer programs (software) that typically run on dedicated hardware (also commonly called servers) that provide services to other computers and users. It is important to know what type of server you are interested in and clearly communicate that to a client to avoid any confusion (for example, when referring to a "database server," do you mean the database program, the hardware that hosts the program, or a combination of the two?). There are many types of servers; some intended for user use such as Web servers or file servers (File Transfer Protocol or FTP servers), some for application use such as backend database servers, and some for networking purposes such as Domain Name Servers (DNS) or network time synchronization (Network Time Protocol or NTP servers). Every server uses a unique logical port to listen on to receive and service requests. Thus, multiple software server executables can operate on a single hardware server. Network traffic can be identified based on the specific port that is in use during a communication session.

Virtual private networks (VPNs) are a software- or hardware-based solution for protecting data as it moves across unprotected networks. A VPN functions by encrypting data between the two endpoints of a communication session so that any listening device with access to the traffic can see the movement of the data but cannot unscramble the message. VPNs can be set up in a permanent fashion, such as between two office buildings of an organization, so that all traffic between the sites is protected, or on an ad hoc basis, such as when a traveling sales rep connects back to the home office to upload customer orders.

All network devices must be capable of passing control and status information between the various devices. The sophistication of this software can vary from very simple control programs to complex operating systems. For example, Cisco Systems networking equipment uses software known the Internetwork Operating System (IOS). The more complex the device (i.e., the higher it operates in the OSI model) and the more tasks it must perform, the more sophisticated the controlling software must be and the more robust and expensive the hardware must be. The configuration of the network software for the various devices involved in a network audit should be a key area of focus and should be consistent and well-documented across an organization. One key issue to keep in mind when reviewing network operating systems is that the software was typically not designed with access by multiple users in mind. Frequently the only user to be considered was a single network administrator who by virtue of their job role would be expected to have administrative access. This results in most network devices having poor logical controls and can lead to a compromise of the device if an unauthorized user is able to gain physical access to the device and simply restart the system.

All of the devices involved in a network need to be interconnected in some manner, and the interconnections take both logical and physical forms. Physical topology refers to the actual cabling of devices, while logical topology refers to the manner in which the devices are organized and relate to one another. The most common topologies are ring, bus, star, tree, and mesh.

Chapter 6: Networks

In a ring topology, devices are connected by unidirectional transmission links. The links form a closed loop and do not connect to a central interconnecting device. Each node in a ring network is dependent upon the preceding nodes, and in a simple network, if one node fails, all other nodes are affected. This shortcoming is frequently addressed through the use of redundant rings operating in opposite directions, one clockwise and one counterclockwise. If one ring fails, the other ring takes over. Another approach to address the weakness with a ring topology is to use a star topology at the physical layer and a ring at the logical layer. A ring topology is illustrated below:

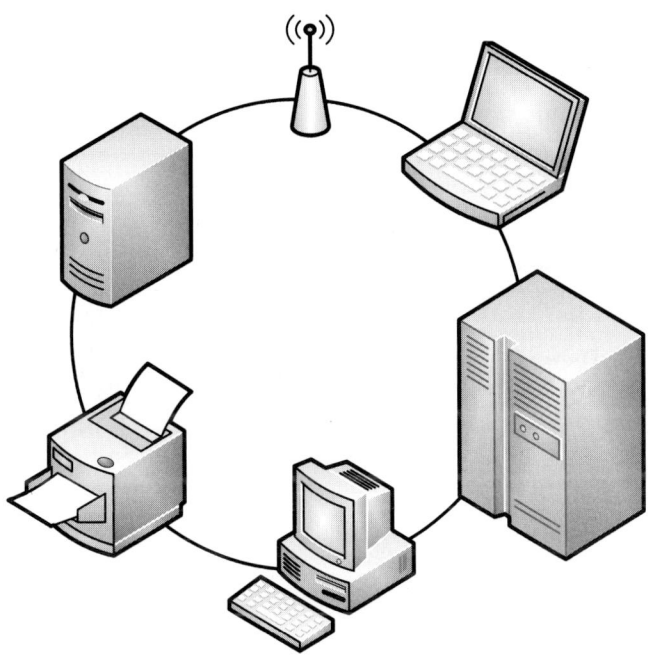

101

Bus topology uses a single cable running the length of the network with nodes attached to it at drop points. Each node listens to the cable and decides to accept, process, or ignore each packet that passes down the wire. If a single node fails in a bus topology, it does not necessarily affect the other nodes; however, if the cable is broken, it will sever communication between systems that end up on different cable segments. A bus topology is illustrated below:

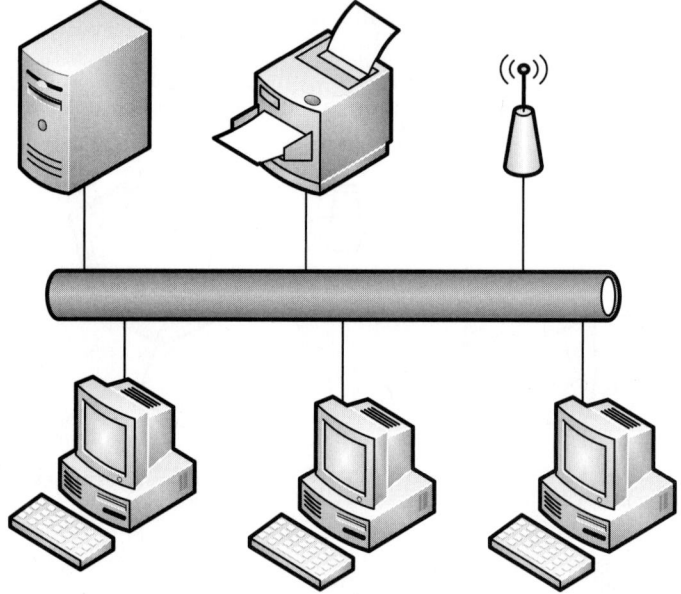

The star topology is found most commonly at the outer edges of complex networks where most nodes connect into the network, and as the basic design structure of simple networks. In a star topology, all nodes connect to a central hub or switch with their own dedicated link. Because each node is attached independently, a failure of any node is isolated from all other nodes and does not impact the network. Because all nodes are connected in to a central device, that device becomes a potential single point of failure, and its failure will impact the entire network. A star topology is illustrated below:

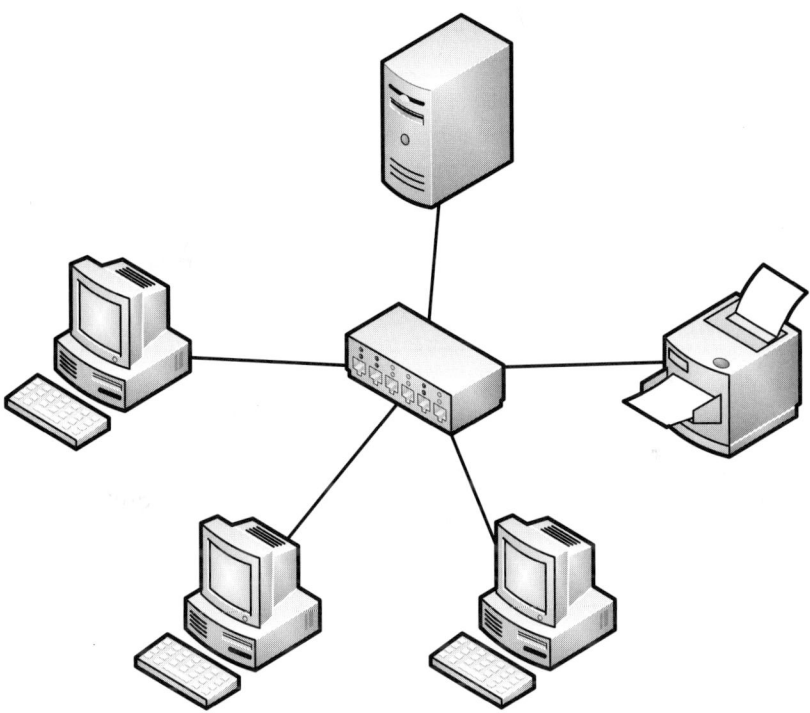

A tree topology is also commonly used in designing simple networks and is a hybrid of both the bus and star topologies. A tree design connects groups of star-configured networks to a central linear bus backbone. A tree topology is illustrated below:

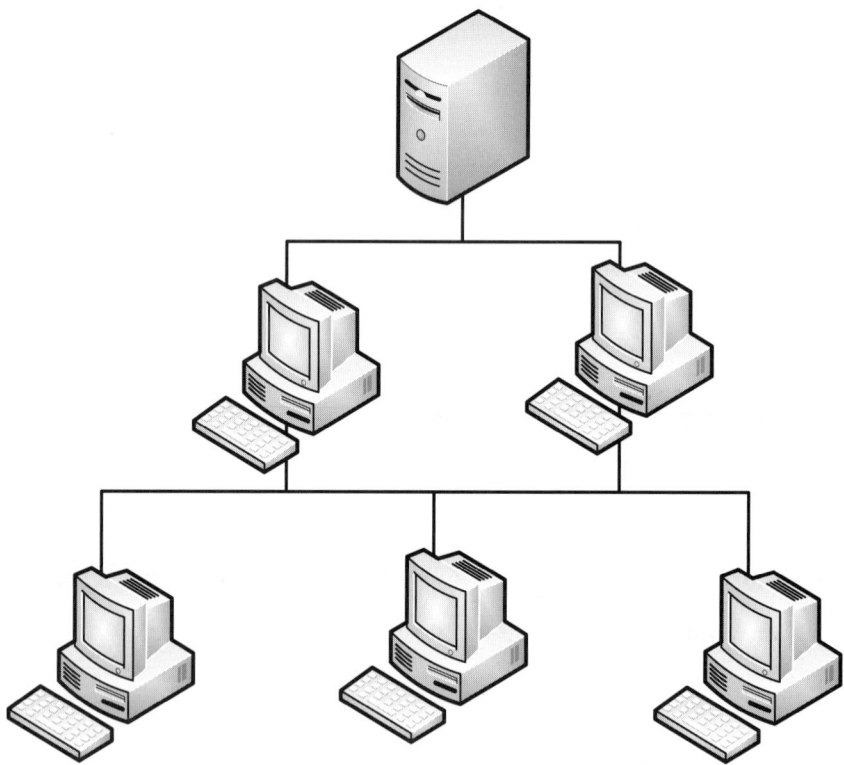

A mesh topology is the most complex and expensive network design structure and is typically reserved for backbone networks that connect other networks together. A mesh network is considered to be either partial or full mesh depending on the robustness of the redundancy designed into the connections. In a full mesh, every system is directly connected to every other system. A full mesh network requires $(N*(N-1))/2$ links to fully connect all nodes. A partial mesh links some systems to all other systems and some systems to only a few other systems. A full mesh network is illustrated on the following page:

Chapter 6: Networks

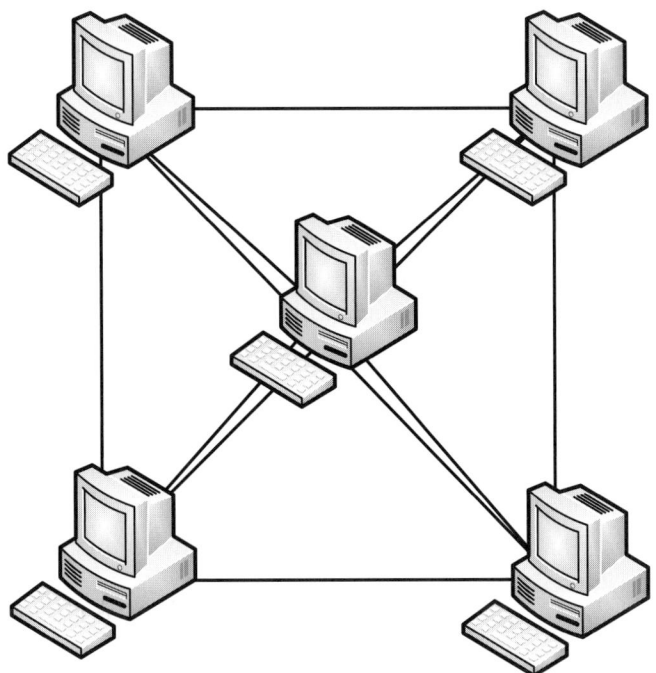

All of these interconnected devices are organized into logical groupings of machines when considered from a functional, geographic, or responsibility perspective. Some of the more common groupings are local area networks (LANs), wide area networks (WANs), demilitarized zones (DMZs), extranets, intranets, and even the Internet.

A LAN is typically a small collection of systems that reside in a single location or are entirely under the control of a single entity, though "small" is a relative term and can contain hundreds of systems or more, depending on the size of the organization. For example, an organization might have a finance department on one floor of a building, an accounting department on another floor of a building, and a few people from the human resources department sitting on both floors. They can organize their network into two physical LANs, one on each floor with all nodes on each floor connecting to independent switches, and then connect the two switches together with a bus to form a tree network. They can then logically segment their two physical LANs into three networks by configuring their switches to prevent people in the finance and accounting departments from seeing any of the network traffic related to the human resources department. This segmentation is known as a virtual local area network (VLAN) because it is done at a logical layer (layer 3) and not

105

the physical layer (layer 1). Because the organization has sole responsibility and complete control of the network environment, it can be a highly trusted environment when architected correctly.

A WAN connects LANs that are geographically dispersed, or that are not under the control of a single entity. If, in the previous example, the organization also owned a building on the other side of the country and ran a cable between the two offices to send its data back and forth, it would most likely be considered a WAN, but more likely it would lease the transmission media from a communications carrier to provide the long haul movement of data. The organization would have no responsibility for the equipment between the sites and would not exercise control over the carrier's activities or decisions. Also, the protocols used to transmit data over WAN links are different than those used for local networks and the transmission speeds tend to be slower. Because the organization has no control over the telco environment, the WAN link would be considered an untrusted (or at best partially trusted) environment, and data moving across that segment of the network would be considered to be at a higher risk than data transiting solely on the LAN.

A DMZ is special network segmented from the main business network to provide resources to entities over which an organization exerts little or no control, such as customers, vendors, or the general public. This segmentation allows the organization to employ additional controls and restrict access to increase the security of its core systems and still allow untrusted or partially trusted access to a limited set of resources. Typically, systems such as Web servers, e-mail servers, and file transfer servers are found in a DMZ. A DMZ is usually established through the careful deployment and use of routers and firewalls to control traffic into and out of the subnet.

An extranet is a logical construct that provides much of the security found in a DMZ, but is set up to connect to other organizations with which an organization has an ongoing relationship and some specific need to link their systems together on a more permanent basis. An example of this would be an automotive manufacturer that creates an extranet to connect to a parts supplier with whom it has regular ongoing business to check inventory levels, place orders, and monitor delivery status.

An intranet is a restricted access network that operates on the same principles as the Internet (that is, it uses Web technologies) but is not connected to the true Internet. Intranets are frequently used within an organization to provide

Chapter 6: Networks

for the sharing of information such as policies and procedures, employee social events, or other non-critical business activities.

The various relationships between network devices and connections are captured in a network topology diagram. Frequently within an organization there are many diagrams showing various levels of detail and various types of relationships. There are cabling diagrams, subnet diagrams, DMZ diagrams, and others. When talking about the "architecture" of a network, typically one is referring to the design goals of the network, while the topology addresses how the network is actually constructed. A simplified logical or architecture diagram of the functional relationship between network elements in a very simple organization might look as follows:

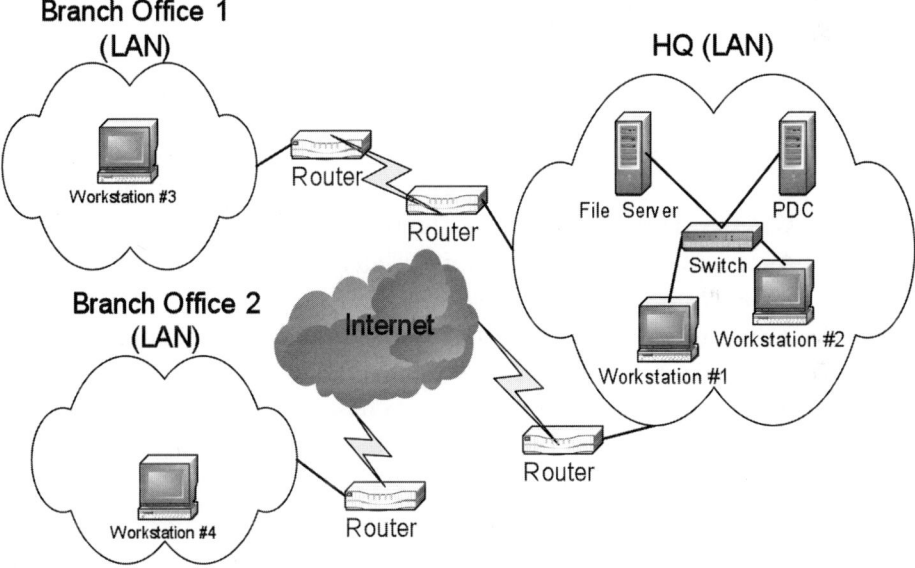

A network topology is the starting point for planning a network audit as it helps the auditor to visualize and understand the complex structure and relationships in the environment. Network design diagrams also provide a point of reference when discussing control design and implementation with network administrators.

The key points of focus when performing a network audit are:

- Network design.
- Network configuration.

107

- Network administration.
- Network change management.
- Network performance monitoring.

The general areas of risk most relevant to networks are:

- Damaging exposure to critical systems.
- Costly downtime.
- Reduced productivity.
- Access to sensitive data.

Typical examples of control activities that might be found in a well-designed and operated network could include:

- Network security and change management policies and procedures have been documented.
- Appropriate authentication is required to gain access to the network, including the use of passwords that are changed periodically.
- Privileged level access to the network (i.e., modify configuration, system privileges, user accounts) is appropriately restricted.
- Access to the network is appropriately approved and documented before such access is granted.
- Access to the network is removed timely for users who have changed roles, transferred, or been terminated.
- Auditing is enabled to record and report security events.
- Firewalls have been implemented to provide protection against external connections.
- Network scans are performed periodically to detect any potential vulnerability.
- Network changes are documented, tested, and approved before implementation.
- A supported version of the network operating system is installed and vendor-supplied updates are applied timely.

Some questions to ask during a network audit include:

- What network services are allowed?
- What network operating software is currently in use?
- Who or what team is responsible for network administration?

- What software is currently used to assist in configuration management and patch management?
- What software is currently used to monitor network availability and performance?
- To what extent are wireless networking capabilities used across the organization?
- Have standards (baselines) been developed?
- How is access to routers, firewalls, and network servers controlled?
- Is a separate "shadow" or out-of-band network used for administrative connections to network devices?
- Are the password settings on network devices in compliance with the global password policy?
- Who has access to change the network configuration?
- How is the confidentiality of IP addresses maintained?
- How is access to diagnostic ports on network servers controlled?
- To what extent is encryption used within the network?
- Does network configuration documentation also denote how and why various ports are used?
- How often is testing performed to help ensure that unused ports are monitored and restricted?
- To what extent are procedures for network implementation, administration, and maintenance documented?
- How is network administration handled in the organization? Is there a separate group for routers/switches and firewalls?
- How do network administrators authenticate to network devices?
- Are intrusion detection systems installed?
- How often are security and auditing logs reviewed and investigated?
- How are the passwords to generic accounts maintained?
- How is the company website maintained?
- Has all network and communications equipment been labeled to assist vendors and technicians with maintenance?
- To what extent are network change management procedures documented?
- What defines a change that is subject to the change management methodology?
- How often are new devices added to or removed from the network?
- Who approves network changes and modifications?
- What requirements have been established for testing network changes?
- What is the current version of the network operating system?
- How are vendor updates (i.e., patches) identified and evaluated?

- How often are patches applied?
- Have performance standards been established?
- How is performance against those standards monitored?
- To what extent does capacity planning take place?
  - Does it include an analysis of such things as average message length, protocols used, transaction volume per server, and message traffic volume?
- How does the network support team review new applications to determine their impact on existing systems?

Documentation that could be useful to review during the course of a network audit might include:

- Network diagrams.
- Network baseline configuration.
- Emergency change process documentation.
- Performance monitoring and capacity planning documentation.
- Security and monitoring procedures.
- List of network services performed by external parties.
- Security listing of individuals with privileged level access to network devices.
- Key configuration files for network devices.
- Security auditing reports containing events generated from the intrusion detection system or network devices.
- Results of network security scanning tools.
- Evidence of the version and patch level for software.
- Population containing network changes in the audit period.
- Sample of network change request forms.

CHAPTER 7

OPERATING SYSTEMS

Sample Risks	Sample Control Activities
Operations: Poorly configured system parameters slow or prevent user access to key business applications.	• Current, supported versions of operating systems are installed, including all necessary patches, updates, and external drivers. • Logging and troubleshooting utilities for system performance are installed, active, and regularly monitored by system administrators.
Security: Unauthorized access to a system results in exposure, loss, alteration, or destruction of sensitive and/or regulated information.	• Appropriate authentication is required to gain access to the server, including the use of passwords that are changed periodically. • Privileged (i.e., administrative) access to systems is restricted to authorized individuals and all critical activities are logged and monitored. • Operating system access is appropriately approved and documented before such access is granted. • Access is removed in a timely manner for users who have changed roles, transferred, or been terminated. • No application programs are allowed to run in a privileged state.

Sample Risks	Sample Control Activities
Change Management: Changes to the operating system create vulnerabilities, cause applications to end abnormally (also known as an *abend*), or cease functioning entirely.	• Operating system security and change management policies and procedures have been documented. • Vendor patches and updates are tested and approved in an offline environment before deployment on a production system and a backout plan is available. • Systems software changes are adequately tested with associated applications to ascertain adequate compatibility and functionality. • Systems software changes are initially installed and evaluated in a test environment before implementation in the production environment. • Critical system libraries and directories are configured with read-only access. • Modifications to the operations schedule must be appropriately approved. • Access to production processing control language and executable programs is appropriately restricted. • Requests for changes to systems software are documented and approved by management before implementation into production. • Designated emergency accounts have been established for granting production access in emergency situations.

Chapter 7: Operating Systems

Operating systems, also known as systems software, are collections of programs, utilities, and supporting computer code that act as an intermediary between users and applications and the underlying hardware that makes up a computer and its attached devices (known as peripherals). An operating system is the most important program that runs on a computer, because without it the computer would be useless. The operating system is loaded into real memory (discussed later) shortly after the computer boots up or starts, and takes over the responsibility for controlling access, operation, and management of the computer. This abstract layer between the user (either human or software) and the hardware provides a common platform to which application developers can write programs that provide user functionality without having to worry about managing and communicating with all the various different types of printers, monitors, system memory management, processor scheduling, and other mundane operational tasks. Operating systems handle activities as diverse as recognizing input from a keyboard, to sending output to a monitor, to keeping track of where various files are stored and which users can access them.

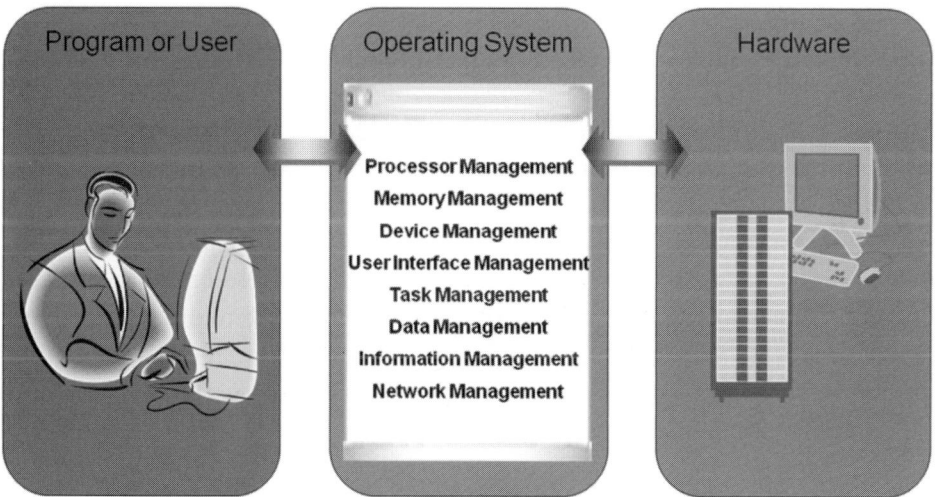

Fig. 1 – A Simplified View of Operating System Interactions

Although all operating systems appear to perform essentially the same functions, they do so in very different ways. Most major operating systems have been in existence for quite some time, so the fundamental structure of an operating system often dates back many years, and in some cases, many decades.

Current versions of different operating systems may appear to be quite similar to one another while only vaguely resembling their own ancestral roots, but they likely have substantially different architecture, design assumptions, and control structures. The longer an operating system has been in existence the more likely it is to have absorbed and implemented elements from a variety of other operating systems, while newer operating systems try to take the best ideas of existing operating systems and fuse them into even more powerful and flexible environments. The result of this evolutionary process is that there is not a straight-forward, clearly defined example of a typical operating system. There are, however, some common generalities that allow us to broadly categorize different types of operating systems based on certain functional or design elements. These common classifications are helpful when identifying potential risks to which a particular operating system may or may not be subject, as well as typical approaches that may be implemented to address those risks.

Common types of operating systems based on design considerations include mainframe, network, server, and client. Mainframe operating systems are used in centralized environments with all users tied to the central processing unit (CPU) of the core system by "dumb" terminals and depend on the host for processing capabilities. Some common IBM mainframe operating systems are MVS, OS390, z/OS, and VMS. Network operating systems have no centralized locus of control or single point of failure; rather they are conglomerates of multiple systems sharing responsibility for managing the environment and distributing functionality in a redundant manner. Examples of network operating systems are Novell Netware and Microsoft's Active Directory. Server-based operating systems are found in decentralized environments but control a single host, with various service functions distributed across different hosts to spread the workload and optimize the performance of individual systems. Some common server operating systems are Unix, IBM OS/400, and Windows Server 2003. Client operating systems are those that run on user devices, typically PCs, which can perform some independent processing and are used to communicate with the servers in a distributed client/server environment. Common client operating systems are Windows Vista, Apple's OS X, and Unix. The most frequently performed reviews include mainframe, network, and server operating systems. Although the users of applications have client operating systems that reside on their user devices such as laptops, the ability to impact the overall system environment is fairly limited.

When determining what operating systems are relevant to the audit, this begins with identifying the risk and scope. If the audit is intended to include related general computer controls for a certain application, the auditor will need to consider the related hardware/servers in scope, along with the associated operating systems. Although various operating systems will be related to the application, the auditor should evaluate the risk associated with each environment and prioritize accordingly if there is limited time and resources. The following is an example where the various operating systems supporting an application are identified:

Server	Operating System
Database Server	Unix
Application Server	Windows Server 2003
Web Server	Windows Server 2003
User Devices (PCs)	Windows Vista

Functionally, operating systems are typically either batch-oriented or interactive, and single-user or multi-user in nature. Batch-oriented systems collect information and actions over time and then submit them for processing at some point in the future. Interactive systems process events as soon as they occur and respond to the user immediately. Because batch-oriented tasks are typically run with system-level privileges, a common risk is that an unauthorized request or transaction will be inserted into a batch job and then be executed with elevated authority as though it were legitimate. Single-user systems are only capable of handling processing tasks for one user at a time, while multi-user systems can handle processing for many users simultaneously. A common risk in poorly secured multi-user environments is the possibility of users viewing or accessing files, information, or transactions of other users without authorization.

As an illustration of some of these concepts, imagine a typical online banking scenario: a bank customer (using a client operating system such as Windows 95, which is a single-user system) connects to a Web application server (perhaps running HP-UX unix) operated by the bank for electronic banking activities. The customer submits an instruction to transfer funds from a savings account to a checking account. The Web server responds instantly with a transaction number and a confirmation that the transaction has been completed, an example of an interactive session. Behind the scenes, the Web application server has passed the information to the bank's backend mainframe which runs their Loans & Deposits software and is used by all the bank employees (a multi-user system). The mainframe collects the customer's transaction request, along with similar requests from any other customers in a queue or holding area, until at a certain point in the future (perhaps based on time, volume, or performance load) it submits all the requests in one batch to update the balances of the various customer accounts. Until the update occurs, the bank's authoritative financial accounting system and the customer have different values for the balances in the customer's checking and savings accounts (although the net funds on deposit are equal). If this inconsistency is not captured and tracked by the bank somehow, there is a risk that the bank's account information will not reconcile with the customer's confirmed activity.

Essential activities performed by any operating system typically include:

- Processor management.
- Memory management.
- Device management.
- User interface management.
- Task management.
- Data management.
- Information management.
- Network management.

The activities can be categorized by whether they are physical or logical in nature. The first three activities (processor, memory, and device management) are all physical operating system functions, while the remaining five activities (user interface, task, data, information, and network management) are all logical operating system functions. It can be helpful (though an oversimplification) to think of the eight areas as concentric circles, like an archery target or an onion, with each layer depending on the services provided by the circles within it to perform its functions. The most frequently used or core services of the operating system are in the kernel of the OS. The kernel is the part of the operating system that is loaded into real memory when the computer is powered on and remains in real memory at all times. Less used services, such as those provided by device drivers, can be loaded and unloaded from memory as needed.

As mentioned previously, each layer of the OS provides specific services related to the physical or logical resources of the system. The layers do this primarily by accounting for the status of the resource they are managing, allocating the resource to a user or program when requested or available, and recovering the resource when the user or program is finished with it. For example, the parts of the operating system responsible for processor management control the CPU. Processor management divides time into discrete slices and allocates those slices to various tasks waiting to be processed by the CPU based on their priority. Once one task completes or reaches the end of its time slice, the next task is given access to the processor. By rotating the tasks being executed, the OS gives the appearance that many tasks are being executed simultaneously (multitasking) when in fact it is simply high speed sleight-of-hand and the apparent simultaneous execution of tasks. This is only an illusion created by the processor management elements of the operating system.

Memory management controls and allocates access to the various types of memory used by a computer. To differentiate between the concepts of physical and logical events in the computing environment, the following example using memory management helps distinguish the two concepts. The physical part of memory management is concerned with the total amount of random access memory (RAM) installed in a computer and managing the reading of data from and the writing of data to the physically installed memory modules, while from the logical side, memory management organizes the available memory space into a series of equal pages (typically 4K in size but configurable by the system) and assigns them as needed for program executable code and data storage. A user's program is given the illusion that it has been allocated enough contiguous memory to execute the entire program and its associated data when in reality the data can be randomly scattered across pages in various locations. In the event there is not enough real (physical) memory available to completely load a program or its data, a tactic is used whereby less used pages in memory are reassigned to active processes and the previous contents written to virtual pages stored on the hard drive. This is what is known as being "paged out" for later recall. The primary difference between the real memory, which represents the actual physical capacity of the silicon chips in the computer, and the virtual memory, which is actually specially allocated space on the hard drive, is access speed. Items stored in real memory are immediately available for processing, while items in virtual memory have to be read from the hard drive into real memory before they can be processed.

Device management in the context of an operating system controls all activities involved with accessing and operating any hardware connected to the system other than the CPU and real memory. Essentially this means anything connected to the input/output (I/O) bus (communications channel) such as disk drives, printers, keyboards, monitors, network interface cards, modems, etc. The operating system uses "device drivers," pieces of code specific to each type of device (and frequently to each brand and model of device), to talk to each device. This element of the operating system is used by the logical management elements of the operating system such as data management to, for example, access files on a disk drive. Given the extraordinarily large number of peripheral manufacturers and types of peripherals, it is not possible for an operating system vendor to write drivers for every piece of possible equipment that could be attached to a computer (not to mention devices that have not been released at the time of the operating system release). As such, operating system vendors tend to write generic drivers that will provide basic services for broad classes of devices. Manufacturers of peripheral devices frequently write their own drivers to be included with the installation of their equipment that "hook into" the operating system for operating systems that do not have the capability to interact with their devices or to include enhanced functionality. Many OS vendors also bundle the most common drivers for a number of vendors with their software, even if the devices are never attached. Given the close interaction of the core operating system with device drivers, it is easy to see how a change to one or the other of the pieces of code could have a significant impact on the functioning of the unaltered element. For this reason it is important for an organization to have documented procedures for the connection of any new hardware or the installation of any new device drivers.

User interface management is the part of the operating system with which a user interacts. There are two typical methods for a user to interface with a computer: through the use of a command line where instructions are typed at a prompt and through the use of a graphical user interface (GUI) which uses graphic elements such as buttons and icons to instruct the computer. While these two methods may seem significantly different, in fact they perform essentially the same function and it is just the appearance to the user that is different. A GUI can be thought of as generating commands similar to those that would be typed on a command line and transferring the request to the operating system transparently. Clicking on a Print File button in a GUI has the same effect as typing the command "print file" on a command line — both instruct the computer to send the contents of a file to a printer through the use of a print driver. Command-driven user interface management that is performed with a mainframe operating system often refers to a green screen due to the text color and background.

Chapter 7: Operating Systems

Task management works hand in hand with processor management, receiving a request by a program to be executed and evaluating the program to determine its execution priority. If the program is an interactive task, it will receive a higher priority than one that is a batch task. Task management sets up the task, gets it ready for execution by calling memory management to allocate memory, and then loads the program. Once the task is released to processor management, it is executed based on its initially assigned priority.

Data management deals with the file system and the logical storage of data. When a file needs to be written or read, the application program makes a request to data management, which stores the details as to physical location and characteristics of the file. This information is used by data management to form a request to device management to get or put the data from or to the desired device (disk drive, CD, etc.). Note that data management does not actually control any devices, but uses the services of device management in processing the data. Data management uses a series of tables and lists that contain information about the files that are stored, such as the date they were created, what device they reside on, the physical location of the data on the device, the size of the file, etc. There are many file systems in use and all have strengths and weaknesses depending on the purpose for which they are used. In the Unix environment, the inode map is commonly used. An older Windows approach includes the file allocation table (FAT), which was replaced by NTFS. Also, some IBM mainframe systems use virtual storage access method (VSAM). The important concept to keep in mind is that although many solutions have been developed for the management of data by a computer system, they are all attempting to solve the same problems. Each solution may be more or less successful, and have more or fewer flaws to contend with, but ultimately they are performing the same task.

Information management monitors and records the activities and uses of the entire operating system. Typically, this component is responsible for generating and recording the performance, messaging, and error logs as well as access and security logs. All of the other components of the operating system have the ability to send messages to the information management component, which then either records or discards the information depending on the configuration of the system. Typically, there are a variety of message types that are categorized by criticality to the operation of the system and they have names such as debug, informational, warning, critical, error, etc. The amount of information captured and stored by the system logs can be critical in troubleshooting intermittent or complex problems, but must be balanced with an understanding of what can reasonably be reviewed and stored.

Network management is responsible for the communication of the system with other computers connected via network connections. Network management determines the type of activity that is appropriate, the construction of the communication packet, the address of the other machine, and sometimes the route to be taken for the communication. Network management forms the message to be sent and then requests device management to send the message, usually via the network interface card (NIC). This component of the operating system is commonly referred to as the "network stack." Certain aspects of the network stack can be configured to optimize performance, such as the size of data packets to be constructed, the amount of time to wait before a connection is assumed to be lost, and how many times to retry a lost connection. The tuning of network parameters can significantly impact the performance of a system.

Now that you have obtained an overview of the activities performed by an operating system, we can put it all together in an example. The commonly performed activity of starting a word processor and opening a document by double-clicking on a specific file icon would look like the following:

1. The user requests an application program be run that reads data from a file by double-clicking on the file icon. This process occurs within the purview of the user interface of the operating system.
2. The request to execute the program is sent to task management, which assigns a priority to the task — because this is an interactive task, it is high priority.
3. Task management requests memory management to assign virtual memory to the task and queues the application startup request. At this point, memory management copies the executable program into virtual memory on a disk drive.
4. Processor management examines the eligible tasks, selects the one with the highest execution priority (in this case, our word processor startup request), and executes that task. The program executable code is loaded into real memory and the executing task runs to the end of its time slice or until it needs input or output servicing (for example, it needs data from a disk file), or the task completes its execution. Processor management begins to execute the word processing executable code necessary to start the program.

5. If the task needs I/O servicing, it is handed over to the data management component of the OS, which looks in a set of tables to find what disk drive the data resides and the physical location of the file on the drive.
6. Data management calls device management to fetch the data contained in the desired file off the disk drive.
7. Once the data is brought into real memory, the task again becomes eligible for execution and processor management continues to give it time slices until the task completes.
8. When the task is finished executing the user interface, it is updated with the appropriate information and the user request is satisfied. To do this, user management requests device management to update the information displayed on the screen.

The reason the task is offloaded in step 5 is that the process of physically reading and writing data from a device is extremely time-consuming in terms of processor cycles. The CPU can more efficiently attend to other tasks while waiting for the requested data to be returned.

Areas of risk and control of most concern to business organizations as implemented in operating system environments typically relate to user controls (i.e., creating, managing, and monitoring users), data controls (access rights to data structures within the environment), and program controls (access to the execution of code within the environment). Most operating system vendors configure system default settings related to the operation of the various OS components and the integrated control structures to enhance and support ease of use and flexibility in meeting the performance and operating demands of as many potential customers as possible. These typically lax defaults are the source of many control weaknesses, vulnerabilities, and "best practice" listings and recommendations for modified settings. One prudent approach to addressing this common risk is to have a documented configuration baseline specific to the organization's needs that can be applied in an automated fashion to all new systems before deployment. This approach is sometimes known as the use of a "golden image," which is used as the starting point for the configuration of all similar systems. The configuration of any deployed system can be compared to the values for the golden image (either manually or through the use of an automated testing tool) and any deviations identified, validated, and documented.

As mentioned in Chapter 3, "Risk Assessment," user accounts can exist at all layers of the technology environment: networking, operating systems, databases, and applications. As there is rarely any need for a typical business user to interact directly with the operating system, the only user accounts that should be found are generally associated with employees in the IT function and accounts created by the applications and databases residing on the hardware, which is controlled by the operating system. However, it is quite common to find user accounts at the operating system level. This depends on how the applications and databases interact with the operating system. If users do have accounts defined within the operating system, this typically does not include access to make any changes to the operating system, as this is generally restricted to the IT function. This approach, however, varies by the type of operating system — mainframe environments due to their centralized nature tend to have all of the individual users defined to the system and all user controls are managed from the operating system level. The most common method of simplifying the management and control of users in both centralized and decentralized environments is to place users with similar functions, access needs, responsibilities, or other common characteristics into "groups," each of which allows for the simultaneous management of many users, greatly simplifying the effort needed in large environments. One of the most important concepts in managing users is the "Principle of Least Privilege," meaning that each user and group is assigned only the minimum level of rights necessary to perform their function. One risk to the principle of least privilege is that a user may be assigned to multiple groups (particularly over time) that will allow a collection of rights to accumulate that jeopardizes the basic concepts of segregation of duties and accountability.

All operating systems are responsible for managing and presenting information, typically stored in a system structure known by a variety of names based on the operating system, but commonly called files or data sets. The individual files (or whatever the appropriate name for the system to be audited) are frequently grouped into logical structures, commonly called directories or libraries, to simplify management and security. Typically, these groups are simply just entries in a system data structure or table and have no relation to the physical location of the information. For example, in a Unix environment, a directory is simply a special type of file that contains the names of other files and some information about them. All files (including directories) on a system are owned by someone, either the system itself, an application, or a user. The owner of a file has all authority over the file and can grant rights to the file to other users of the system. The specific rights vary by operating system, but typically have to do with the ability to view the information, write or alter the information, and delete the information. Who has been granted these various rights, and over what objects, is a major component of any operating system audit. Because of the thousands upon thousands of files on any one system, a good way to review file rights is to use an automated third-party tool or utility provided by the operating system.

The function of all operating systems is to provide an interface layer between users, the applications they use, and the hardware that performs the computing activities. The applications that are installed on a particular system, including those that make up the operating system itself, are simply special types of files containing executable code rather than user information. The code that gets executed are sets of instructions created by programmers that request the operating system to perform specific activities such as "open a file" or "print a document." The concern with programs is that the code files cannot be read by people as they have been compiled or converted to a binary machine language that only the operating system can understand to optimize their performance. This means that it is not possible to determine whether a set of instructions (program) is telling the computer to perform the appropriate actions (imagine if a program instruction were "erase all files" — the system might comply and erase everything, including itself), whether a program has been altered, whether a particular program should be on the system in the first place, or if a change to an existing program will cause unanticipated consequences. Because of these concerns, change management is a critical aspect of any operating system audit and should be reviewed to determine the level of adherence to a standardized, documented methodology. Additionally, operating systems have various classes of programs that run differently on the system. These classes are typically grouped into privileged programs that are part of the operating system, batch programs that run unattended, and detached or service programs that run without a user interface, as well as user programs.

Privileged programs run with system-level privileges and are part of the operating system. No user program should ever run in a privileged state, and no privileged programs should be directly accessible to users. Privileged programs execute powerful machine-level instructions and should be carefully monitored by system administrators. Batch programs are not accessed by users directly; they are controlled by an automated counter or timer that initiates the program periodically when certain conditions are met. The purpose of batch programs is to move activities that may consume large amounts of processor effort to a time when it has minimal impact on users and interactive tasks. Because batch programs run unattended, the scheduler is an important audit consideration to avoid unauthorized jobs being inserted into the processing stream. Service programs run continuously in the background of a system, waiting for a request from a user to which they respond. Common examples of these types of programs relate to Web servers and e-mail servers. They do not have to be started because they are continuously available, but they do not do anything until a user connects to them. Because service programs are constantly available, only those necessary for business purposes should be active, and any unnecessary services should be disabled. User programs are initiated by a user, such as a word processor, or those with which a user interacts, such as a payroll processing application.

All operating systems come with some tools to help manage and monitor the environment. The information generated by these tools can be used by the auditors as well during the course of their fieldwork. Some vendors have collected groups of these tools into useful utilities to simplify management of the environment. For example, newer Microsoft operating systems have a tool known as the Security and Configuration Analysis Tool (SCAT), which is a template that compares a number of important system values with recommended settings. In the IBM AS/400 and iSeries environment there are utilities such as System Services Tool (SST), SECTOOLS, and others as well as direct commands to extract information from the operating system. For IBM's AIX (a variant of Unix), there is the System Management Interface Tool (SMIT). For mainframe environments, there are add-on security tools such as IBM's RACF and CA's ACF2 and TopSecret. These tools provide access control and auditing abilities for mainframe systems. In addition to the tools provided by operating system vendors, there are many third-party tools, available for free and for purchase.

There are organizations, both for-profit and nonprofit, such as the Center for Internet Security (www.cisecurity.org) and the Computer Emergency Response Team (CERT) that publish standards and tools that can be used in an audit of operating systems. A good resource for both auditors and systems administrators to monitor for newly discovered weaknesses in their environment is a tool provided by the Center for Education and Research in Information Assurance and Security hosted at Purdue University and found at Cassandra. cerias.purdue.edu, which monitors and consolidates the information from several security tracking services. Additionally, the U.S. National Institute of Standards and Technology through the Computer Security Resource Center (http://csrc.nist.gov/checklists/repository/index.html) provides a number of technology focused checklists that can help formulate specific audit programs, and the U.S. Defense Information Systems Agency (http://iase.disa.mil/stigs/ stig/index.html) provides Security Technical Implementation Guides that

Chapter 7: Operating Systems

provide detailed information about a number of environments. The U.S. National Security Agency (http://www.nsa.gov/snac/) provides a number of Security Configuration Guides at their System and Network Attack Center.

One critical note is that auditors should never install and run tools in the environment they are auditing. Rather, the tool should be tested as any other piece of software and a request should be submitted to install the tool on the system to be audited as any other change would be processed. The tool should be operated by a systems administrator under the supervision and observation of the auditor.

The key points of focus when performing an operating system audit are:

- Operating system acquisition.
- Operating system configuration.
- Operating system access control and administration.
- Operating system change management.

The general areas of risk most relevant to operating systems are:

- Complexity of systems software and the size of the code base comprising an operating system.
- Flexibility and extensibility of operating systems to run code such as Java and .NET that were not anticipated by the original developers.
- The interconnected nature of systems in an organization, causing a local failure to have a ripple effect and impact remote systems.

Typical examples of control activities that might be found in a well-managed and controlled environment could include:

Operating system configuration
- Appropriate authentication is required to gain access to the server, including the use of passwords that are changed periodically.
- Auditing is enabled to record and report security events.
- No application programs are allowed to run in a privileged state.
- Operating system logs are configured to capture important performance and operating information, and the logs are reviewed regularly.
- Logging and troubleshooting utilities are installed, active, and regularly monitored by system administrators.

Operating system access control and administration
- Privileged-level access to the server (i.e., modify configuration, system privileges, user accounts) is appropriately restricted.
- Operating system access is appropriately approved and documented before such access is granted.
- Access is removed timely for users who have changed roles, transferred, or been terminated.
- Critical system libraries and directories are configured with read-only access.
- Designated emergency accounts have been established for granting production access in emergency situations.

Operating system change management
- Operating system security and change management policies are documented, approved, and current.
- Operating system changes are documented and approved by management before implementation.
- Current, supported versions of operating systems are installed, including all necessary patches, updates, and external drivers.
- Vendor patches and updates are tested and approved in an offline environment before deployment on a production system, and a backout plan is available.
- Systems software changes are adequately tested with associated applications to ascertain adequate compatibility and functionality.
- Modifications to the operations schedule must be appropriately approved.

Some questions to ask during an operating system audit would include:

- On which operating system(s) do the relevant in-scope applications and databases reside?
- Is a current system software inventory, including version and last update, maintained?
- Who is responsible for operating system configuration, administration, and maintenance?
- How is the need for system software updates monitored?
- How do administrators keep abreast of the latest security vulnerabilities?
- To what extent is a test environment used to assist in implementing new systems software or updates and performing ongoing maintenance?

- Are there various versions of the current operating system installed on various servers?
- Are there plans to update the current installation and implement a more recent version?
- How are new system software needs communicated to management?
- What procedures exist to support operating system software acquisition and implementation?
- Have operating system standards (baselines) been developed?
- Are the operating system password settings in compliance with the global password policy?
- Is the configuration consistent on the various servers throughout the organization?
- Are configuration changes subject to the change control process, requiring approval and testing and appropriate corresponding documentation?
- Who has administrator-level access to operating systems in place?
- To what extent are procedures for operating systems implementation, administration, and maintenance documented?
- What are the tools used for performance, capacity, backup security, and so forth?
- What nonuser access exists?
- Where are the passwords to generic accounts maintained?
  - Who knows the passwords?
  - How often are they changed?
  - Are the same passwords used across all servers?
- How often is access monitored?
- To what extent are change management procedures documented?
- What defines a change that is subject to the change management methodology?
- Who approves changes and modifications?
- Is testing performed and documented for all changes?
- Are businesses notified of updates that may cause outages?
- What operating system versions and current patches are in place?
  - How are patches identified and implemented?
  - To what extent is configuration documentation updated to reflect system software updates and maintenance performed?
- Are there any system software versions in use that are no longer supported by the vendor?
  - What controls are in place to help ensure that this software adheres to necessary performance and security standards?

- What procedures exist to help ensure that the new system software and existing systems do not conflict?

Documentation that could be useful to review during the course of an operating system audit might include:

- Emergency program change documentation.
- Programming standards for systems development and maintenance activities.
- Listing of software and hardware purchases.
- Listing of systems software development projects.
- System configuration files.
- Population of operating system changes (i.e., patches, configuration changes).
- Sample of change request forms.
- Evidence that the change was tested before implementation.
- Security reporting identifying accounts with access to change the system configuration.
- Security reporting identifying accounts with access to modify user access privileges.

CHAPTER 8

DATABASES

Sample Risks	Sample Control Activities
Operations: A hardware or performance issue prevents access to the database timely by users.	• All mission critical databases are deployed in a redundant replicated manner on parallel systems. • DBAs regularly monitor the performance reports and statistics for their systems to perform maintenance and upgrade systems proactively.
Security: Unauthorized access to a database results in exposure of sensitive and/or regulated information.	• Privileged (i.e., administrative) access to databases is restricted to authorized individuals and all critical activities are logged and monitored. • Database auditing and logging is implemented for all DBA activities and the logs are stored on a separate system.
Change Management: Changes to the database structure result in the loss of critical business information.	• All changes to a database are tested and approved in an offline environment before deployment on a production system and a full backup is available before a change is implemented. • Business unit owners potentially impacted by the change are aware of the pending change and participate in the testing process.

Methods to organize, store, and access information have existed since long before computers became prevalent in business, or have even been in existence. In a simple sense, a file cabinet with four drawers labeled A-F, G-M, N-S, and T-Z with file folders inside each drawer for the related letters of the alphabet is a structured information system that allows for the easy location and retrieval of any piece of data residing within it — in essence the very implementation of the concept of a database. So what, then, is a database?

A database is most easily understood as an organized collection of related information that has some relevance to its intended audience. The key word here is "related." Data (the pieces of information stored in a database that on their own have no intrinsic value) needs to have some connection or relation to other pieces of data and be organized in a logical manner to be considered a database. So a database contains an aggregation of data into records or files that have some relevance to users, such as sales transactions, inventories, customer profiles, purchase orders, etc. Simple databases can be created and maintained with pencil and paper or, commonly in many organizations, with the use of spreadsheet programs.

Larger, more complex databases with more robust and potentially flexible relationships require specialized software to manage the structure of the database environment and the controls over the data as well as a specially trained individual known as a database administrator (DBA) to manage the environment. The software used by a DBA is known as a database management system (DBMS). A database manager provides its users with the capability to control read/write access to the databases containing tables, queries, stored procedures, and other components that make up the data storage architecture, specify report generation related to management concerns (e.g., system access, event logging, etc.), analyze usage of the system, and create and define new types of data structures (for example, an invoice or an employee).

People frequently conflate or confuse the term database with the concept of a database manager, which can lead to miscommunication in the course of an audit if not clearly understood. A typical example of this is when an individual refers to "the Oracle database" when they mean "the financial records tables contained in the database managed by the Oracle software." We will discuss the actual components of a database shortly, but first it is important to understand the different types of database management systems, their evolution, and their intended purposes to understand the concerns the database environment poses to the internal auditor.

Chapter 8: Databases

A number of approaches to addressing the problems of organizing, storing, retrieving, securing, and maintaining information with computer systems have been developed over the past 50 years. The most commonly encountered today are file system-based, relationship-based, and object-relational-based. Each has evolved from the lessons learned from other, preceding approaches, advances in technology, and new business needs. The simplest, earliest of these models is the file system approach.

A file system-based database is basically a collection of large flat files of predefined size and structure that have records written sequentially and have no capability for indexing. This means that a file must be defined and created before it can be used to store data. When the file is created, a programmer specifies the length and layout of the record format and the number of records the file can hold. For example, a customer master table intended to hold all information related to the customers of a business might have a record layout consisting of 80 characters of information related to each customer, with the first 10 characters used to store a last name, the next 10 characters used to store a first name, the next 20 characters used to store an address, the next 10 characters to store a city name, the next two characters for a state, the next five for a zip code, the next 12 for a work phone, and the final 11 for a fax number. The programmer would specify that the file should be capable of holding up to 1,000 records and a file would be created on the system (meaning the hard drive would reserve space for 80,000 bytes of information) and made available for users. Each new customer would be written into the file as they were obtained and their information would be truncated to fit the allotted space if too long, or empty space would be left if more space was allotted than needed. For short last names, this is an inefficient use of space but not a significant potential problem. For customers with last names longer than 10 characters, the record will at least inaccurately reflect the customer information. For two customers whose last names match the first 10 characters and then are different, there is a possibility of incorrectly substituting one customer for the other.

Another problem is encountered when the business exceeds 1,000 customers — they have nowhere to store the information. Also, there is no index of the information in the file; that is, there is no information about where in the flat file a particular record resides. Because the records are sequential rather than ordered and there is no way to keep track of where they were put, each time a particular record needs to be recalled, the entire file must be searched until the specific requested item is found. Later implementations of this design approach improved some of the risk concerns and performance issues, but the design itself has inherent limitations that cannot be overcome. The flat file approach is still deployed widely as it is frequently found on mainframe systems that have been supporting critical business applications for many years (commonly called legacy systems).

A more flexible approach to structuring and managing data is known as the relational model. Unlike the traditional flat file model, which is design driven (the data must fit into the pre-developed structure), relational databases are data driven. They are designed to adapt to the data (long lastname or short lastname is not a constraint on the system design or data storage) and accommodate the relationships between the pieces of information so that the structure of the database can be changed without significantly affecting the majority of data stored within the database.

The key to a relational database is the description of the types and relations of the pieces of information that when combined make up a record. For example, in the customer master file example above (called a customer master table in the relational environment), a record consists of a customer last name and first name that when combined (hopefully) make up a unique combination allowing you to identify a specific customer. Each customer has an address (known as a one-to-one relationship), state, etc., and two possible phone numbers (known as one-to-many relationship). It is these relationships, "one-to-one," "one-to-many," "many-to-many," etc. that typify a relational database. If the combination of the first and lastnames does not provide the ability to uniquely identify individual customers, a key can be assigned to each record as it is created that is unique (for example a five-digit sequential number).

The key can then be used to uniquely identify individual records with the database and create an index, which is a separate table that stores a limited amount of information about the main table that will allow for faster lookups of specific information. If we think of a big table made of rows (called tuples) and columns that intersect at points (called elements) that contain discrete pieces of information of a particular type (for example, the State column), we can see that some data elements will be repeated multiple times. For example, although there may be 10,000 customers, there are only 50 possible states, so many of them will appear multiple times in the table. To optimize the design and efficiency of a database, designers look for such occurrences, remove them from the table, and store them in a separate table, replacing the original data with a unique identifier (known as a foreign key) in the original table. In this example, the 50 states could be removed and replaced with a number between one and 50 (depending on the state), and a list of states could be maintained in a second table where each number assigned becomes the unique primary key for the entry. Whenever a state was needed during retrieval from the original table the database would know to go and look up the related entry in the second table based on the various keys and relationships found in the database and return a record containing a combination of information from the two tables.

As shown in the graphic below, every table relates to at least one other table, and the information in any one table can be modified (or the table structure itself can be changed) without the need to change any other part of the collection. Because data is retrieved by table name, field name, and row number, there is no need to scan entire files or tables for information, thus significantly improving response time and efficiency. A collection of tables along with any associated indices, queries, reports, etc., taken as a whole, is the basis for a database that is managed by a DBMS.

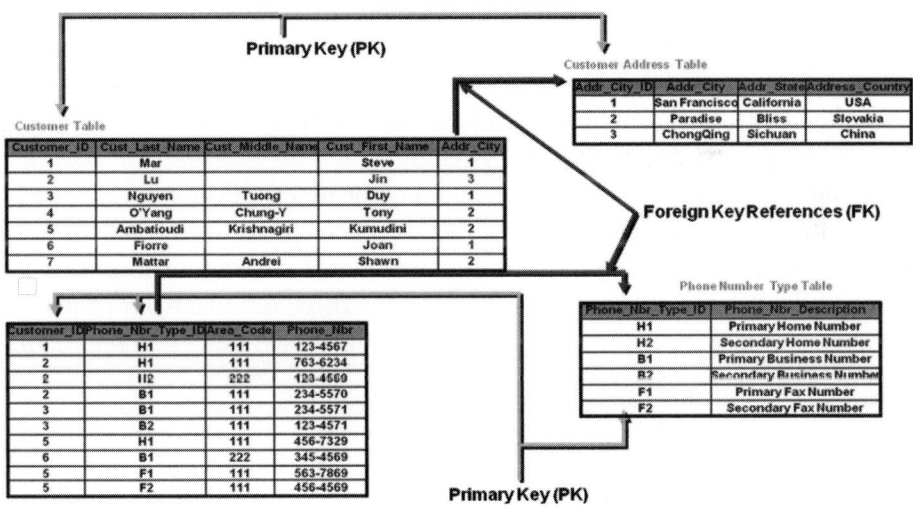

Fig. 1 – Sample Database Relational Structure

Object relational databases expand on the design structure model of the relational database and add the capability to store objects in addition to simple text-based data. An "object" is something that has a "name" that uniquely identifies it, "attributes" that describe it (column names), and "methods" that are applied to the object, that is, actions applications can perform on or with the object. An example of an object would be a song in the iTunes store — it is not a simple piece of data, rather it is an audio file with attributes such as "artist," "length," "size," etc. and it can be purchased or played. Object relational databases (and object-oriented programming languages) most closely capture and store the real-world representations of things as we see and use them. They are, of course, also capable of storing simpler text-based data as well. They also use one-to-one (1:1), one-to-many (1:M), and other similar relationships to describe the structure of the elements that make up the database.

Databases can be made available to users in a number of ways. For example, older mainframe applications may have had flat file types of databases written into the code that makes up the application. More recent databases tend to have the database separated from the applications that use the information they store, both for ease of maintenance, performance, and security purposes as well as to make the data more widely available to any application that might have a need for the information. Breaking up the core components of a system in this way also allows for changes at one layer to be made with minimal impact on the other layers, just as breaking up the tables in a relational database helps minimize and isolate the impact of any changes. The most common architecture used to deploy databases these days is the three-tiered structure. There is a separate layer for the database that typically resides on its own hardware in a distributed environment or frequently is found sharing hardware platforms in mainframe and mid-range environments, a dedicated application server, again typically on its own hardware for client/server systems or sharing hardware on mainframes, and a user interface layer where users actually interact with the "back-end" systems, either through a browser, a dedicated client application, a direct terminal connection, or some other means of accessing and interacting with the system.

This separation of data, application, and user interface allows each platform to be optimized to suit its purpose, but also introduces additional complexity into the environment that must be addressed and managed. Each hardware element can be from a different manufacturer, each operating system can be a different type, and each piece of software deployed can be from different vendors. Although such flexibility and choice allow for a variety of solutions to be optimized for a particular organization, it requires the auditor to have a detailed understanding of all of the pieces before starting an audit, and to work closely with database, system, and application administrators to help ensure coverage across all impacted areas of a database environment as well as the communications layers between all of the components. It is also critical

Chapter 8: Databases

to accurately understand the scope of the audit so that the fieldwork does not start crossing into related but out-of-scope areas.

Because access to the data stored within a database is a critical concern to many businesses, a number of ways to help ensure availability have been devised. The most common are parallel servers, replication, and backup and recovery schemes. Parallel servers address the risk by creating multiple instances of a database running on multiple servers located in multiple locations. If anything should happen to one server, the others take over transparently and no impact is noticed by the users. This type of high availability solution is complex to implement and run but provides excellent protection for mission critical environments with time sensitive needs. Replication, on the other hand, is not as responsive in terms of failover time and a delay can be experienced, particularly if the process has a manual component. Replication does, however, provide a robust recovery as a copy of the live database is replicated frequently to other machines to reduce the risk posed by an isolated database as a single point of failure. There may be some impact to the timeliness of the database as some records may have been modified between the time of the last replication and a failure, but the impact is usually minimal. Backup and recovery schemes can provide recoverability for non-mission-critical databases, but because the time between backups is typically large, any failure would require a significant effort to recreate all the records lost at the time of a failure.

It is important to differentiate between the data structure (tables) and the data values (entries in tables). The first is related to the database management system and the second is related to the databases themselves. Risks exist at both levels and each should be evaluated. There are some subtle differences that exist between risks and controls associated with managing data, and those associated with managing a database, that help differentiate which item one is reviewing. Risks and controls for data tend to focus on integrity, ownership, confidentiality, and similar concepts, while risks and controls related to a database are more focused on change control, access security, availability and reliability, and similar concepts. Because databases are critical to an organization, they are typically subject to stronger change management controls than other elements of the technology environment; however, one risk that this introduces is uncontrolled replication of sensitive information. Because a test environment needs to mimic the conditions of a production environment, it is common practice to capture a copy of live production data and then populate it into a test environment to provide realistic scenarios. The concern is that if any of the information is of a protected nature, the programmers and developers working in the environment may see data which is legally restricted. This is a result of what is known as data aggregation — the concept that isolated pieces of information on their own are not valuable; however, as the information across tables and databases is viewed and connected, or aggregated, the combinations can add up to form a protected class of information. For this reason, live production data, if absolutely needed in a test environment, should be used in a strictly controlled manner.

Due to the constantly changing nature of the information within a database as it is accessed, updated, modified, altered, and created throughout the course of the day, it is difficult to capture static images of the environment that can be used for recovery if changes are made to the environment that result in unanticipated consequences. Even automated change management tools have a difficult time addressing the complex, fluid nature of the database environment. This makes database maintenance and updates risky activities that should be guided by well-documented policies and procedures.

A key area of focus during the audit of a database is user access and how users authenticate to the system to gain access. As mentioned earlier, users can be defined at any or all layers of the technology stack, frequently in multiple places simultaneously. This should cause increased concern in a database environment as data is typically one of the most valuable assets a business owns. Databases permit access to users through one of four methods: operating system authentication, network authentication, database authentication, or application authentication. The terms define what resource management function the database will accept validation information from. In a database using database authentication, it maintains its own user tables and access rights tables and users are authenticated directly to the database. Because most users, with the exception of DBAs, have no need to access the underlying structure directly, there should be few if any users granted this level of access. Operating system authentication means the database looks to the operating system tables of authorized users and accepts any user who is defined to the operating system. Network authentication relies on an external source to validate a user's request for access. The database may rely on a single sign-on solution, a hardware-based token, centralized user management system, or other solution. Application-based authentication is typically the most common method provided for users. A user account is controlled by the application and access to the database is by the application on behalf of the user. This reduces the exposure of the database to a minimum number of accounts and allows for easier monitoring of database activities.

Regardless of the approach used to authenticate a user, an important aspect of the environment to evaluate is the permissions and privileges granted to users and the implications of the combination of the two. Permissions are items in the database to which the user is given access (for example, a particular table) and privileges are those actions the user may perform on the item, such as add/change/delete. The principle of least privilege (as previously described) applies to databases and should be carefully examined during an audit. Frequently used combinations of permissions and privileges can be combined to create roles, a template that can be granted to a user to simplify management similar to the concept of groups in the operating system environment.

Because the primary function of a database is to store and manage data, it is an ideal tool to use for system logging and reporting and can be used for all sorts of captured activities and events. In fact, many databases come with robust auditing capabilities related to their own environment and can capture an immense amount of information related to their performance, activities performed or requested by users, modifications to stored data, and many other potentially useful pieces of information. Databases are capable of capturing and retaining so much information that fully logging the entire environment has the potential to impact the performance of the machine running the database as well as overwhelm the individuals and tools responsible for monitoring the logs. Database auditing is a benefit when correctly implemented and configured, but it must be designed carefully. One common concern is a DBA's access to a database and his or her authority over the items contained therein. If the database logs are contained within the database, they cannot be considered reliable when it comes to recording and reporting the activities of the DBA, because the administrator would have both the motive and the opportunity to alter the information. A better solution for database logging is to capture the information on a remote system to which the DBA does not have access, and assign responsibility for reviewing the logs to an independent party, such as a security function.

Some key terms to become familiar with related to the database environment:

- Distributed database — Component database elements reside physically in different locations but are logically connected to represent one main database.

- Data dictionary — A central repository that describes the data elements within a database and their relationships. A data dictionary is an example of metadata, that is, data that describes other data.

- Stored procedures — Frequently performed database activities can be scripted and saved so that they can be run as a single reference. Commonly they are used to automate administrative tasks and should be appropriately secured.

- Triggers — A trigger is an event on the system that has been specified beforehand to be monitored for, and when it occurs the system takes a specified action. For example, a trigger could be established for the size of a system log. When the log exceeds that size, a trigger references a stored procedure that compresses the log and moves it offline.

- Data ownership — The practice of assigning responsibility for the security and integrity of critical business data to specific teams or individuals for regular monitoring and approval of user access.

- Data warehouse — A central repository for all or significant parts of the data that an enterprise's various business systems collect. Typically, a data warehouse is used for strategic purposes and tends to be relatively static over time (the data is not volatile).

- Data mart — A repository of data gathered from operational data and other sources, which is designed to serve a particular community of knowledge workers. Typically, a data mart is used for tactical purposes and the data may change or be refreshed frequently.

- Data mining — Sorting through data to identify patterns and establish relationships. Commonly used to search data warehouses and data marts, the results of which are often referred to as "business intelligence."

- Data modeling — The analysis of data objects that are used in a business or other context and the identification of the relationships among these data objects.

- Structured Query Language (SQL) — A standard interactive and programming language for getting information from and updating a database. Although SQL is both an ANSI and an ISO standard, many database products support SQL with proprietary extensions to the standard language. Queries take the form of a command language that lets you select, insert, update, and locate the data, among other things. There is also a programming interface for SQL. A common source of confusion in the database environment is the use of the term SQL (which is a language) as shorthand for Microsoft's MS SQL product, which is a database management system.

- Data Definition Language (DDL) — language that is used for metadata (data that describes other data) used to define the structure of the database such as "Add Table," "Drop Table," "Create User" and similar instructions affecting the design and structure of a database environment.

- Data Manipulation Language (DML) — language that is used to manipulate information within the database structures, such as "Insert Row," or "Delete Record."

Key points of focus when planning a database audit are:

- Database design.
- Database configuration.
- Database administration.
- Database change management.

The general areas of risk most relevant to a database audit are:

- Accuracy: The database is the record of all the transactions accounted for by the organization. If input or processing controls render any of this information inaccurate, the credibility of the financial statements, support for business decisions, the ability to meet legal obligations, and other critical business functions can be affected.

- Data corruption: The database contains master data, which is the source for every transaction accounted for by the organization. If master data is corrupted for any reason, then each transaction using that data is invalid.

- Timely access: If performance issues impede the timely access to databases, all of the applications and processes that rely on the information will be impacted. System outages can result in costly downtime with business activities disrupted until the issues are corrected.

- Data protection: Many types and combinations of data are regulated and protected in today's business environment, and the frequent movement across shared mediums can expose data to unauthorized individuals or entities and result in legal, monetary, or reputational damage to an organization.

Typical examples of control activities that might be found in a well-managed database environment could include:

- Database security and change management policies and procedures have been documented.
- Appropriate authentication is required to gain direct access to the database, including the use of passwords that are changed periodically.
- Privileged access to the database (i.e., modify database configuration, system privileges, user accounts, and table data) is appropriately restricted.
- Activities using privileged access (e.g., DBAs) are monitored and/or performed with adequate management supervision.
- Access to the database is appropriately approved and documented before such access is granted.
- Access to the database is removed timely for users who have changed roles, transferred, or been terminated.
- Auditing is enabled to record and report security events; the logs are reviewed periodically to detect security violations.
- Database changes are documented, tested, and approved before implementation.
- Supported versions of the database are installed and vendor-supplied updates are applied timely.
- Vendor default passwords are appropriately modified upon installation.

Some questions to ask during a database audit would include:

- Describe the current data architecture of the application systems currently in use.
- What types of database management software are in use?
- To what extent are procedures for database implementation, administration, and maintenance documented?
- Is the DBA team appropriately staffed?

- Have appropriate tests been planned and performed specific to the database upon system installation?
- Are data owners assigned to monitor the security and integrity of the new data?
- What database integrity mechanisms are in place for the databases under review?
- Have database standards (baselines) been developed?
- Are the database password settings in compliance with the global password policy?
- Does the database distinguish between DBA and non-DBA profiles for passwords and other login requirements?
- Describe any direct database interfaces or open database connectivity (ODBC) connections.
- Is the configuration consistent on the various databases being used by the organization?
- How is database administration handled in the organization?
- To what extent are procedures for database implementation, administration, and maintenance documented?
- How is database access managed?
- What nonuser access exists?
- Are database tools used for administration?
  - What are the purposes of the tools (performance, capacity, backup security, etc.)?
- Where are the passwords to generic accounts maintained?
  - Who knows the passwords?
  - How often are they changed?
  - Are the same passwords used across all databases?
- How often is database access monitored?
- Which users have the ability to update application databases directly and why?
- Are there any audit trails on changes made directly to the database?
- How often is the database backed up?
- Are scripts used to monitor database activities such as performance and data backup?
- To what extent are database change management procedures documented?
- What defines a change that is subject to the change management methodology?
- Who approves database changes and modifications?
- Is testing performed and documented for all database changes?

- Are business users involved in updates that are made to the database?
- What has prompted the need for database maintenance or modification?
- Is the data dictionary updated automatically for any changes to the database?
- What is the current version of the database?
- How are the DBAs notified of vendor updates (i.e., patches) to the database software?
- How often are patches applied?
- Has there recently been an upgrade or conversion that requires a migration of the data to a new version or a new server?

Documentation that could be useful to review during the course of a database audit might include:

- Diagram of current database architecture.
- Listing of all databases and the applications they support.
- Listing of all database interfaces.
- Policies and procedures relating to database implementation, administration, and maintenance.
- Database standards/baselines.
- Data dictionaries/schemas for existing databases.
- Listing of data owners.
- Database configuration files.
- Reports listing profiles and users with access to the database.
- Database monitoring reports.
- Listing of users with access to database monitoring tools.
- Listing of generic accounts and users who know the passwords.
- Database scripts that perform critical activities.
- Listing of database changes.
- Sample of database change request forms.
- Testing/conversion plan and associated results.

CHAPTER 9

APPLICATIONS

Sample Risks	Sample Control Activities
Operations: Data being transmitted between two applications as part of a shared transaction environment is altered, erroneous, or incomplete.	• Calculated values related to the data to be transmitted such as hash totals, checksums, or other comparison values are automatically generated before data transmission and recalculated after data transmission to ensure complete and accurate data transfer. • Applications use unique identifiers such as sequential numbering to prevent duplicate transfers of data.
Security: A user creates unauthorized or fraudulent transactions.	• Only authorized users are granted access to business applications, the access is role-based using the principle of least privilege, and such access is reviewed periodically by management. • Transaction logs are automatically generated and reconciled by an individual independent from the activity performed.
Change Management: An update to the application environment results in a loss of business functionality or access.	• All changes to production applications are tested in a separate environment by both the IT function and the business units engaged with the application before implementing any change.

Sample Risks	Sample Control Activities
Change Management: An update to the application environment results in a loss of business functionality or access. (cont.)	• All production changes are governed by detailed procedures that include a component to ensure the ability to revert to a prior state should evidence of an unsuccessful change be encountered (this is often referred to as "backout" procedures). • All application system changes are tested and approved before implementation into production.

Application systems are why computing has become as prevalent in the business world as it has. It is the applications that automate repetitive, standardized activities and significantly increase the productivity and accuracy of employees in an organization. Applications are the reason for the hardware, operating systems, databases, and supporting IT processes. Without them, the rest of the IT environment has no value to a business.

Application audits occur at the intersection of business processes and technology, and how they are scoped is key to the value they deliver to an organization. Application audits must address risks inherent in both the business process and the use of technology as well as risks introduced by the use of technology to enable the business process.

There are three main types of application processing encountered in a business environment: batch processing, online processing, and real-time processing. Batch processing collects transactions as they are generated and holds them until a certain trigger is reached, commonly either a minimum number of transactions, a certain amount of time passed, or a particular time of day. At that point, the transactions are all processed as a "batch." An example of this type of environment would be a payroll check processing run. Checks can be entered throughout the week and then late on a Thursday night, when the system is not being used for anything else, the checks can all be printed. Batch processing is commonly used to reduce the system load when other users may need access or when the activity is not particularly time sensitive.

Batch processing can be triggered either manually or automatically. Online processing is an interactive mode of performance in which the application performs activities directly at the command of a user, such as releasing an electronic purchase order directly to a vendor when the user presses the enter key at the end of data entry. Real-time processing occurs without the need for a user to be present during the process (for example, when an electronic order is received from a customer and the system automatically checks inventory levels and generates an item pick list to be shipped by the warehouse department).

The most logical and efficient method to perform an application audit is to trace or test each of the transaction types and the various actions that can occur to them through the application, noting the performance of all the control mechanisms, both manual and automated. An effective method to perform the tracing process is to "walk through" a typical transaction as it goes through the system. In the walkthrough, discuss with business unit staff what edits or changes may occur to the transactions at each step in the process. While they may not explicitly call the controls system edits, ask questions around how transaction limits, thresholds, data input accuracy, and other transactional controls are enforced. In many cases, this enforcement will be through application system edits.

An application audit can follow a business process (e.g., payroll) through one or several applications, programs, or modules across the application layer, or can be confined to a single program (e.g., time-keeping) throughout the entire IT "stack." An application audit also can encompass several programs across all layers of technology, but then runs the risk of becoming overly complex or suffering from "scope creep." If an application audit is performed from a business process or transaction perspective, the results will likely need to be taken into consideration in conjunction with the results of a general computer controls audit to provide reasonable assurance regarding the audit assertions being attested to as each technology layer relies on the layers below it to perform adequately. Less experienced IT auditors sometimes overlook critical elements in the IT infrastructure, particularly databases. Remember, the majority of application systems will rely on at least one database (e.g., Oracle, DB2) to operate, and access to this layer of the system needs to be assessed at some point as well.

Unfortunately, the large number of different business transactions with their associated variety of activities, when taken into consideration with the multitude of vendor and in-house developed application solutions available, makes a business process perspective at anything more than a general level beyond the scope of this text. However, there are many application risks and control concerns that are more generic in nature and can be performed from a technology perspective rather than a business perspective. These include controls related to the transfer of data between information systems as transactions (regardless of type or platform) are processed, access to the underlying code structure of the applications and their related maintenance, and auditing and monitoring activities, for example. The most common areas of generic application controls (in addition to those related to technical activities such as change control) are those related to the input, processing, storage, output, and security of information as it moves through an application. Audit logging and information reporting should be included in all five areas. This approach and these elements are the focus of this chapter.

In addition to the occasional manual control that may be encountered during an application audit, the auditor will be focused on the automated controls that are in place. The IIA's *GTAG 8: Auditing Application Controls* describes two types of automated controls: those that are inherent or embedded (also called "programmed") into the application and cannot be altered without changing the underlying application code, such as an edit check that prevents alphabetical characters from being entered into a numeric field, and those that are configurable, such as a tolerance limit for purchase order amounts that can be set by the organization based on their business environment and organizational requirements. A thorough understanding of all of the automated controls available in an application can usually only be found in the documentation of the program, and frequently there are many more than an individual organization has implemented. Here again, it is useful to perform a walk-through encompassing critical transaction flows. In the walkthrough, critical automated controls can be identified by discussing each step of the transaction flow with business unit management in that area. Through this process, the most critical automated controls can be identified and subsequently prioritized for assessment.

GTAG 8 (in referencing *GTAG 1: Information Technology Controls*) states that the objective of application controls is to help ensure that:

- Input data is accurate, complete, authorized, and correct.
- Data is processed as intended in an acceptable time period.
- Data stored is accurate and complete.
- Outputs are accurate and complete.

- A record is maintained to track the processing of data from input to storage and to the eventual output.

These objectives, in addition to data security and user access objectives, are achieved through the use of several types of controls consisting primarily of preventive and detective activities. Again, as identified in GTAG 8 referencing GTAG 1, the types of controls typically found in business applications are:

- Input Controls — These controls are used mainly to check the integrity of data entered into a business application, whether the data is entered directly by staff, remotely by a business partner, or through a Web-enabled application or interface. Data input is checked to help ensure that it remains within specified parameters.

- Processing Controls — These controls provide an automated means to help ensure processing is complete, accurate, and authorized.

- Output Controls — These controls address what is done with the data and should compare output results with the intended result by checking the output against the input.

- Integrity Controls — These controls monitor data being processed and in storage to help ensure it remains consistent and correct.

- Management Trail — Processing history controls, often referred to as an audit trail, enables management to identify the transactions and events they record by tracking transactions from their source to their output and by tracing backward. These controls also monitor the effectiveness of other controls and identify errors as close as possible to their sources.

Each of these control objectives, types, and activities should be considered both before and during the course of a walkthrough to help ensure all areas of concern to the business are being addressed.

Most vendor-provided applications have a large portion of their configurable controls preset before shipment of the application, and unless modified during deployment, remain in their default setting. Unless it has been verified that the vendor value does not pose a risk to the organization, it should be assumed that any default setting is a potential control weakness. Also, when performing the walkthrough, ask business unit representatives if they sometimes perform manual overrides or work around the system controls. This can be indicative of poorly designed automated controls at the least, or a sign of potential unethical behavior at the most.

One of the main advantages of automated application controls over manual business controls is that they are considered to be more reliable, because they are not subject to human judgment or error. Another significant advantage to automated controls from an auditor's perspective is that they do not need to be sampled for testing. When a control is automated, it is considered to be operating in a binary fashion, either effectively or not. This means a selection of one is adequate to form an opinion of the efficacy of a control. The process of determining a statistically valid sample size and selection based on the frequency of a control activity is not necessary to form a conclusion.

A key point of interest regarding application controls is that they depend on the underlying IT general computer controls (GCCs) to maintain reliability (similar to the layers of a network, higher functions in a business application rely on the integrity of lower-level controls). A benefit of this is that if the underlying GCCs are found to be reliable and there have been no changes to the application controls, they can be relied upon to remain in the same state as the last time they were tested. This approach (known as "benchmarking" and described in the U.S. PCAOB's AS5 documentation) can provide considerable savings in both time and money when performing IT audits by allowing an auditor to minimize the amount of time and effort needed to test an automated application control if it has been tested in the past.

The key points of focus when performing an application audit are:

- Project planning and management.
- Systems design and acquisition.
- Systems development and testing.
- Systems rollout and turnover.
- Accuracy of calculations.
- Completeness of processing.
- Change control and maintenance.
- Application administration.
- Application security and configuration.

The general areas of risk most relevant to intended or newly deployed applications are:

- Cost overruns.
- Schedule overruns.
- Less functionality than required.
- Accuracy of calculations and processing.
- Inaccurate or incomplete processing.

Additionally, several areas of technical risks can be experienced with newly deployed applications, including:

- Negative impact on existing legacy systems.
- Incorrect mapping of interfaces (e.g., from a subsystem to the general ledger).
- Incompatibility with existing information security standards (e.g., password parameters).
- Removal of powerful developer or technical implementer access after production.

Typical examples of control activities that might be found in a well-managed application environment could include:

- Application security and change management policies and procedures have been documented.
- Appropriate authentication is required to gain access to the application, including the use of passwords that are changed periodically.
- Privileged-level access to the application (i.e., modify application configuration and user accounts) is appropriately restricted.
- Designated emergency accounts have been established for granting production access in emergency situations.
- Application owners authorize the nature and extent of user access privileges before such access is granted.
- Access to the application is removed timely for users who have changed roles, transferred, or been terminated.
- A periodic (i.e., semiannual) review is conducted to verify that only authorized users have access.
- Auditing is enabled to record and report security events.

- Access to implement changes into the application production environment is appropriately restricted.
- Vendor default passwords are appropriately modified upon installation.
- Application changes are documented, tested, and approved before implementation.
- Application changes are developed, modified, and tested in an environment separate from the production environment.
- Management approves the results of the conversion of data from the old application system or data structure to the new application system or data structure and monitors that the conversion is performed in accordance with management's intentions.
- A supported version of the application is installed and vendor-supplied updates are applied timely.
- Configuration settings that determine flow and processing of transactions (e.g., which general ledger account to debit when an inventory movement occurs) are set in accordance with management's objectives.

Some questions to ask during an application audit include:

- What significant projects have occurred in the last year and what is currently in process for the next five years?
- How are priorities among existing and conflicting projects managed?
- What is the process for reporting status and issues to project sponsors and executives?
- What is the average time issues in the issues log have been outstanding?
- To what extent is a project management team able to choose project team members based on skills and needs (rather than simply availability)?
- To what extent are outside consultants and contractors involved with implementations?
- How have detailed user requirements been identified, documented, and incorporated into design documents?
- To what extent have design specifications been documented:
  - Data files?
  - Interfaces?
  - Procedures?
  - Screens?
  - Reports?

- Have requirements regarding systems development and testing been defined and documented?
- What steps are taken to help ensure that changes made to software packages are kept to a minimum?
- Where changes to software packages are made, what process is in place to help ensure that built-in controls and integrity processes are not compromised?
- To what extent have test plans been developed to facilitate testing?
- Do test plans include volume testing, stress testing, error testing, and testing of all customized features?
- How are changes controlled as systems progress from testing to final approval?
- Have change management policies and procedures been documented?
- Is the application system a vendor-purchased system or an in-house developed application system?
- Are programmers only given access to those parts of the systems necessary for their work?
- Who is responsible for implementing changes into the production environment?
- Are business users involved in updates that are made to the application?
- Is testing performed and documented for all application changes?
- What is the process for monitoring vendor sites for patches, fixes, and upgrades?
- How are application patches, fixes, and upgrades tested and implemented?
- Do separate logical or physical environments exist to develop, modify, and test application changes?
- Is the organization using versions of third-party systems no longer supported by their vendors?
    - How is this monitored?
    - What procedures are in place to monitor these systems to determine if replacement or major upgrade is required?
- What backout and recovery procedures are in place?
- Has there recently been an upgrade or conversion that required a migration of the data to a new version?
- Is there an emergency change process?
- How often are emergency changes implemented?
- Have emergency accounts been created to allow access to the production environment in certain situations?

- How are emergency changes documented, reviewed, and approved?
- How is security access to systems authorized and administered?
- Is there a designated individual within the business who is an IT liaison?
- Who approves access to the application?
- Are there various approvers based on the type of access being requested?
- Does the application administrator receive notification when a user changes positions or leaves the organization?
- What generic accounts exist and how are they maintained?
- Is auditing enabled? If so, who reviews the logs?
- How are the specific values for configuration settings determined and implemented?
- How are changes to configuration settings managed and controlled?

Documentation that could be useful to review during the course of an application audit might include:

- **Policies and Procedures**
  - Application development
  - Error detection and correction
  - Change control and maintenance
  - Operations, technical, and user
- **Change Control and Maintenance**
  - Listing of changes implemented into production
  - Change control forms
  - Listing of individuals with access to migrate changes into production
  - Documentation indicating that non-production environments exist
- **Application Administration**
  - Report with application users and associated access privileges
  - Monitoring reports
- **Systems Development and Testing**
  - Vendor software and support agreements
  - Test plans and associated results
  - Application and security architecture

Chapter 9: Applications

Additionally, if the application being tested is newly implemented or being tested for the first time, one might also obtain the following documents:

- **Project Planning and Management**
    - Listing of projects
    - Status reports
    - Issue logs
    - Project budget and tracking reports
- **Systems Design and Acquisition**
    - Systems development life cycle methodology
    - Capital expenditure authorization form
    - Project request form
    - Statement of work
- **Systems Rollout and Turnover**
    - Implementation schedule
    - Training plan

CHAPTER 10

AUTOMATED TOOLS: USING TECHNOLOGY TO AUDIT

During the course of an audit, an auditor strives to obtain sufficient, relevant, and useful evidence to achieve the audit objectives effectively. The audit findings and conclusions should be supported by appropriate analysis and interpretation of the evidence.

Today's information processing environments pose a stiff challenge for an IT auditor to collect sufficient, relevant, and useful evidence because the evidence exists in non-physical form (e.g., magnetic media). Automated tools are an important means for an IT auditor to gather information from these environments. When systems have different hardware and software environments, different data structure, record formats, processing functions etc., it is difficult for an auditor to collect evidence and analyze records without the use of technology. Therefore, in planning the audit, an IT auditor should also consider computer-assisted audit techniques (CAATs) in addition to manual testing activities. Several types of automated tools are discussed in this chapter, each illustrated through a summary description of some commonly used examples of actual tools.

Automated techniques also enable IT auditors to gather information independently. Automated tools provide a means to gain access and analyze data for a predetermined audit objective and report the audit findings with an emphasis on the reliability of the records produced and maintained in the system. The IT auditor should be very careful about the completeness, accuracy, validity, and reliability of the source data used by automated tools, because doing so provides reassurance regarding the findings generated and the conclusions developed.

As per ISACA, the IT auditor should consider an appropriate combination of manual and computer-assisted audit techniques during the planning of an audit. In this regard, it has also issued guidance as "G3: Use of Computer-assisted Audit Techniques (CAATs)." Similarly, Standard 1220.A2 issued by The IIA emphasizes that "internal auditors must consider the use of technology-based audit and other data analysis techniques" in exercising due professional care.

In deciding whether to use automated tools or not, factors to be considered include:

- Computer knowledge, expertise, and experience of the IT auditor.
- Availability of suitable automated tools and IT facilities.
- Efficiency and effectiveness of using automated tools over manual techniques.
- Time constraints.
- Integrity of the information system and IT environment.
- Level of audit risk.

Steps to Be Undertaken Before Using Automated Tools

The major steps to be undertaken by an IT auditor in preparing for the application of the selected automated tools include:

- Setting up the audit objectives of the automated tool, which may be included in the terms of reference for the exercise.
- Determining the accessibility and availability of the organization's IT facilities, programs/systems, and data.
- Clearly understanding the composition of data to be processed, including quantity, type, format, and layout.
- Defining the procedures to be undertaken (e.g., statistical sampling, recalculation, confirmation).
- Defining output requirements.
- Determining resource requirements (i.e., personnel, automated audit techniques, processing environment [the organization's IT facilities or audit IT facilities]).
- Obtaining access to the organization's IT facilities, programs/systems, and data, including file definitions.
- Documenting the tool to be used, including objectives, high-level flowcharts, and run instructions.

Before using any automated tool, the IT auditor should confirm that the detailed specifications of the tools and all the parameters necessary for

Chapter 10: Automated Tools: Using Technology to Audit

processing selected data have been met. This step is critical to provide reasonable assurance of obtaining the audit objectives. The auditor should:

- Perform a review of the logic, parameters, or other characteristics of the tool.
- Confirm that the automated tool has been installed on an appropriate operating system.
- Review the organization's IT policies to confirm they do not expressly prohibit or discourage use of such tool.
- Determine that the use of the automated tool will not affect the integrity and availability of the data of the organization.
- Evaluate the organization's general IT controls, which may contribute to the integrity of the tool (e.g., program change controls and access to system, program, and/or data files).

The IT auditor should also confirm the following regarding the output generated by automated tools:

- Perform a reconciliation of control totals, if appropriate.
- Review output for reasonableness.

Automated techniques include many types of tools, such as generalized audit software (GAS), utility software, application software tracing and mapping, expert systems, and automated testing tools. In addition to the above, technology also can be applied for documentation and workpaper management and Risk Analysis and Risk Management Software for integrated governance risk and compliance (GRC) types of environments.

A. Generalized Audit Software

GAS refers to standard software that has the capability of reading and accessing data directly from various database platforms, flat-file systems, and ASCII formats. GAS provides IT auditors an independent means to gain access to data for analysis and the ability to use high-level problem-solving software to invoke functions to be performed on data files. GAS contains multiple features such as mathematical computations, stratification, statistical analysis, sequence checking, duplicate checking and re-computations. Typically, the various vendor tools provide similar functionality, but have differing areas of strength or weakness and should be evaluated for alignment with tasks commonly expected to be performed by the intended users. These software tools also may be used for data mining and business intelligence to determine trends that are not readily obvious or to search for anomalies in data sets.

Following are common functions performed by generalized audit software:

File access — Enables the reading of different record format and file structures.
File reorganization — Enables indexing, sorting, merging, and linking with another file.
Data selection — Enables global filtration conditions and selection criteria.
Statistical functions — Enables sampling, stratification, and frequency analysis.
Arithmetic functions — Enables arithmetic operators and functions.

The effective and efficient use of GAS requires an understanding of its capabilities and limitations. When using it to access production data, an IT auditor should take appropriate steps to protect the integrity of the organization's data. When developing embedded audit software routines to collect data for use by GAS, the IT auditor should be involved in system design, and techniques should be developed and maintained within the organization's application programs/systems to monitor use.

Popular examples of generalized audit software are MS Excel®, Audit Command Language (ACL®), Interactive Data Extraction and Analysis (IDEA®), and TopCAATs®.

(i) **MS Excel®**

Excel is one of the most commonly used automated tools. This software has the basic features of data analysis and is user friendly in its application. MS Excel can be used for analytical tests, data management, and analysis reports.

Following are the analytical tests supported by MS Excel:

1. Horizontal and vertical analysis
2. Trend and ratio analysis
3. Performance measurements
4. Statistical analysis
5. Aging analysis

Chapter 10: Automated Tools: Using Technology to Audit

6. Benford's law
7. Regression
8. Monte Carlo simulation

Following are the data management/analysis report functions supported by MS Excel:

1. Append/merge
2. Calculated fields/functions
3. Cross tabulate
4. Duplicates
5. Extract/filter/export
6. Index/sort
7. Gaps/blanks
8. Join/relate

(ii) Audit Command Language (ACL®)

ACL is one of the most extensive automated software tools currently available for auditing. It has the capacity to handle an enormous volume of data and complex transactions. ACL can help an IT auditor in efficient execution of the audit work. Following are the solutions offered by ACL:

- Audit Productivity
- Continuous Auditing/Monitoring
- Fraud Detection
- Regulatory Compliance
- Secure Data Access
- Team Collaboration

a) **Audit Productivity:** Allows IT auditors to directly access all of the source data required for audit analysis using server technology to rapidly analyze a large volume of various types of transactional data. Direct access to source data helps the IT auditor shorten the audit cycles. With ACL, audit scripts allow repetitive tasks to be constructed once and deployed as required on a regularly scheduled basis.

b) **Continuous Auditing/Monitoring:** Allows organizations to determine the effectiveness of key controls by analyzing financial transactions continuously and independently. The major advantage of this solution is a timely insight into control problems; early discovery and reporting of fraud, errors, and inefficiencies; and effective identification of risk areas. It reduces the audit time and effort spent on controls testing, resulting in a more efficient and sustainable compliance process. By embedding audit best practices into an organization's business processes, operational performance gains and increased profitability are attained through correcting control deficiencies, plugging revenue leaks, and improving cost management.

c) **Fraud Detection:** Allows an auditor to run a comprehensive set of tests designed to detect indicators of a wide range of fraud regardless of which IT system houses the transactional data and how many records need to be analyzed. With the ability to test 100 percent of transactions, investigation with ACL can uncover all relevant anomalies — typical signs of fraud, error, or abuse. Through automation, these tests run continuously, often catching the fraud early before the money goes out the door, making remediation easier and acting as an effective deterrent for other potential fraudsters.

d) **Regulatory Compliance:** Allows organizations to comply with various regulations that require management to report on the adequacy of the organization's internal control over financial reporting. ACL provides organizations with a suite of predefined tests based on COSO's framework that are run automatically and continuously to monitor for anomalies in financial transactions.

e) **Secure Data Access:** The secure data interface allows ACL to provide a single point of view to 100 percent of data read directly from corporate databases while adhering to the enterprise's security protocols. This is accomplished regardless of the volume, type, or location of the data. Using ACL, data is kept in a managed and secure IT environment and not on an individual's laptop where it can be exposed to unnecessary risk of loss or theft. Because the data is viewed and analyzed in read-only mode, it cannot be altered or deleted. Eliminating the need for IT to provide data extracts reduces the length of audit cycles, retains the integrity of the data, and removes the burden on IT resources.

f) **Team Collaboration:** Allows a collaborative approach to conducting audits. ACL software allows the knowledge and information typically generated by IT auditors to be shared with the rest of the team. Projects, data, data definition and dictionaries, standard test libraries, and test results can all be stored in a centralized, secure server-based environment. Scripts capturing repetitive tasks can be made available to all team members. The automated logging of audit procedures makes it easy for IT specialists to review the work of their teams. This collaborative approach also extends beyond the internal audit department. Because ACL technology allows direct, secure access to data, the burden of creating and updating data extracts for the audit teams is removed from the IT department. Additionally, as the data remains in the secure server environment, adherence to security and data administration standards, a key IT objective, is maintained.

(iii) Interactive Data Extraction and Analysis (IDEA®)

IDEA's functionality can be used to improve performance and extend an IT auditor's capabilities. IDEA can perform the following functions:

- Create a record of all changes made to a file (database) and maintain an audit trail or log of all operations (including import) and every audit test carried out on the database. Each entry is tagged with the user ID from the operating systems login ID.
- Import and export data into a multitude of formats, including formats for large mainframe computers and accounting software. It can read and process millions of records in a very short time. There is practically no limit to the number of records that this software can process.
- Compare, join, append, and connect different files from different sources.
- Extract specific transactions, identify gaps (for example, in a check number sequence), or duplicates.
- Profile data by summarizing, stratifying, or aging the files.
- Create useful file statistics automatically.
- Display the data and results graphically.
- Creation of samples using several different sampling methods.

(iv) TopCAATs®

TopCAATs is a new tool available in the market and has the capability of integrating with MS Excel as a ribbon bar in Excel 2007 and a menu and toolbar in earlier versions. This application leverages the advantages of the already existing features in MS Excel for data analysis.

Following are the main features of TopCAATs:

- Storage of engagement detail information and its use by many of the other tools to pre-populate input boxes, and in headers and audit trails.
- Generation of system reports and performance of a variety of tests on system data.
- Gap and duplicate detection.
- Stratification.
- Audit file sampling — random sampling and a monetary unit sampling (MUS) procedures.
- Comparison of two different worksheet's data and identification of changes.
- Identification of transactions that lie at the extremes of a population.
- Toggle "wrap text" on/off.
- Apply three predefined number formats that can be customized by the user.
- Convert cells with formulas to their values.
- Insert a standard workpaper header, including graphics (company logo).
- Conversion of positive numbers to negative and vice versa.
- Obtaining output in a new workbook containing the results of each test for further investigation. The section module summary sheet details the tests that were run, the options that were specified, and the number of records that were identified by each test.
- Inclusion of a screenshot of the input screen to see exactly what parameter was set, providing a full audit trail.

B. Utility Software

Utility software can come in very handy for IT auditors in the execution of their work. Utility software is not typically developed or intended to be used primarily as audit software. It is frequently a tool used by system administrators or programmers, which also provides functionality or information that is of interest to an auditor. However, use of this software requires some amount of care and precaution. Before using utility software, the IT auditor should

Chapter 10: Automated Tools: Using Technology to Audit

confirm that no unplanned interruptions might take place during processing and that the utility software has been obtained from the appropriate system library. The IT auditor should also take utmost care and appropriate steps to protect the integrity of the organization's system and files because these utilities can easily damage both if not applied carefully. Nmap and Bindview® are examples of utility software.

(i) Nmap

Nmap is a network mapping utility commonly used by network administrators and security specialists. Its documentation describes Nmap as a "network exploration tool and security scanner." Using the transmission control protocol (TCP)/Internet Protocol (IP) address, it has the capability to identify any open "doors" or ports that might be available on a remote TCP/IP device. Nmap can be used by an IT auditor to discover computers and services on a network, thus creating a "map" of the network. Using Nmap, IT auditors can discover passive services on a network despite the fact that such services are not advertising themselves with a service discovery protocol. In addition, an auditor can use Nmap for determining various details about remote computers. These include operating system, device type, uptime, and software product used to run a service, exact version number of that product, presence of some firewall techniques, and, on a local area network, even the vendor of the remote network card. Nmap is an extremely powerful tool and one of the most popular security utilities in the open source community available to an IT auditor. Nmap has different kinds of scanning techniques and options available. Each Nmap scan can be customized to be as blatantly obvious or as invisible as possible. Some Nmap scans can forge its identity to make it appear that a separate computer is scanning the network, or simulate multiple scanning decoys on the network. Nmap can run on Linux, Microsoft Windows, Sun Solaris, and Mac OS X.

Main features of Nmap are:

- **Flexibility:** It can support dozens of advanced techniques for mapping networks filled with IP filters, firewalls, routers, and other obstacles. This includes many port scanning mechanisms (both TCP & UDP), OS detection, version detection, ping sweeps, etc.
- **Powerful:** Nmap can be used by an IT auditor to scan huge networks.
- **Portable:** Nmap supports most operating systems, including Linux, Microsoft Windows, Mac OS X, HP-UX, NetBSD, Sun OS, etc.

- **Easy:** Nmap supports both traditional command line and graphical (GUI) versions.
- **Free:** The primary goals of the Nmap project are to help make the Internet a little more secure and to provide administrators/auditors/hackers with an advanced tool for exploring their networks. Nmap is available for free download and also comes with full source code that can be modified and redistributed under the terms of the license.
- **Well Documented:** Nmap has been documented in multiple languages for ease of use by IT auditors.
- **Supported:** Being open source, Nmap is also supported by developers and users, including auditors.

(ii) **Bindview® EMS**

BindView Enterprise Management System (EMS) is a network and resource reporting tool, commonly used by systems administrators. It uses snap-in management modules to collect data from all areas of the enterprise. When the user plugs in a single module for a single NOS (e.g., NT), the module works as a comprehensive management and security tool for a homogeneous network. When it is integrated with multiple modules to manage multiple NOSs (e.g., NetWare 3.x, NetWare 4.x, and NT), BindView EMS lets the modules access information from NetWare or NT from one console and view information from multiple NOSs on one screen. BindView EMS provides an integrated view of enterprise management and security across Windows NT, NetWare, IntranetWare, and Open NDS. This module helps the IT auditor analyze the operating system's security, systems resources, and configuration parameters for both NT servers and workstations. Bindview EMS focuses on security assessment, user account assessment, server, workstation, and application configuration analysis, all of which are tightly integrated within the BindView EMS object-oriented Enterprise Console. This tool helps the auditor in assessing network, hardware, or application anomalies.

C. Customized Queries or Scripts

Customized queries or scripts allow the IT auditor to specifically target desired information from the system for analysis. Customized scripts are highly useful for environments where other automated tools are not available. These queries/scripts usually require specific technical skills to create them. Writing these kinds of queries/scripts requires knowledge of computer languages; therefore, the IT auditor usually obtains the help of a software professional in writing them. The IT auditor explains the output requirement to the software professional and also helps identify the source data. Before placing reliance upon the output generated from these customized queries, the IT auditor should obtain assurance of their integrity, reliability, usefulness, and security through appropriate planning, design, and testing. Customized query and script code should be maintained in a secure location to prevent unauthorized changes from occurring.

D. Application Software Tracing and Mapping

When using application software tracing and mapping, the IT auditor should confirm that the source code being evaluated has generated the object program currently being used in production. The IT auditor should be aware that application software tracing and mapping only points out the potential for erroneous processing; it does not evaluate actual production data. This fact makes the tools appropriate for use both by developers and auditors.

E. Audit Expert Systems

Audit expert systems are specialized tools that can be used to analyze the flow of data through the processing logic of the application software, and document the logic, paths, control conditions, and processing sequences. When using audit expert systems, the IT auditor should be thoroughly knowledgeable of the operations of the system to confirm that the decision paths followed are appropriate to the given audit environment/situation.

F. Document and Workflow Management Software

Document and workflow management software provides control over audit documentation by organizing and storing them securely. These types of applications use electronic cabinets to store audit files and audit documentation electronically. A cabinet is a directory on a local or network drive that contains audit files. An audit file is used to store and organize electronic audit documentation specific to an engagement. When a file is opened in a document manager, the documents are displayed in a hierarchical index structure. All documents relating to an audit, including planning, reporting, workpapers, and trial balance documents, are created and maintained in audit files. Audit documents created electronically can also be edited, copied, and used in subsequent years. This software allows access only to authorized users and provides a complete audit trail of document creation, modification, distribution, and usage. This software is a crucial component of the internal control structure and for compliance reporting under different legislation. This software also interacts with existing business software to conduct and manage an audit and document the processes performed. Document and workflow management software can search and retrieve data from a variety of document types, such as narratives, e-mail and flowcharts, giving the IT auditor the ability to analyze the frequency of internal control activities, categorize the types of internal controls, and test internal controls. Further, such software can rank the importance, materiality, and impact of various risks and internal controls. Beyond documenting the audit tests performed and the audit findings, some software packages include audit planning templates and select audit samples, allow for automated review and approval of audit documents, aid in the generation of audit reports, and recommendations. Document and workflow management software may be Web-based, allowing online audit planning, workpaper management, workflow approval, access to data in a variety of locations, collaboration among audit teams, and communication of necessary information to remote locations. Web-based software must have enhanced security features as compared to stand-alone tools. Examples of document and workflow management software are AllClear Proquis®, Amadeus Compliance Management®, Oracle E-Business Suite®, and RSM McGladrey Auditor Assistant®.

G. Risk Analysis and Risk Management Software

Risk analysis and risk management software assess possible business risks, the potential losses arising from such risks, and existing or recommended controls for risk mitigation. Some packages highlight key risk areas to be monitored and trace key risk performance indicators on a continuous basis. Therefore, risk analysis and management software is a crucial component to assess and document the adequacy of the internal control system for different legislation. To aid the assessment process, risk analysis and management software may contain risk databases of common risks and internal controls for various business processes, while others allow the user to build an industry-specific risk database. To achieve the broadest possible analysis and documentation of risk, this software may have a flowcharting or visual presentation component, ability to survey and receive feedback from employees anonymously, and templates for assessing fraud potential. Software that offers an anonymous survey and feedback capability can be useful to organizations concerned with complying with protection of whistleblower policies.

H. GRC Activities Monitoring Software

The tightening of regulations, increasing pressure from financial markets, and additional compliance requirements have shifted the focus from mere risk management to a comprehensive integrated governance, risk, and compliance framework. Traditional approaches to governance, risk, and compliance have relied upon separate point solutions to address the requirements of each business process and different regulatory requirements. This fragmented approach may at times lead to inefficiencies, added costs, and an inability to maintain compliance initiatives and make informed and accurate decisions. Governance, risk management, and compliance (GRC) provides a useful framework for coordinating many different endeavors to make more risk-informed business decisions. Today, many organizations no longer see these activities as separate; rather, they find that there are a lot of commonalities and interrelationships between the three areas.

Adopting a unified IT governance, risk management, and compliance (IT GRC) approach and managing the associated activities coherently will create efficiencies, provide a holistic view of the IT environment, and help ensure accountability. Within the GRC realm, it is very important to realize that if the first one (governance) is not in place, the second (risk management) and third (compliance) become irrelevant and probably cannot be meaningfully achieved. Working on the same logic, if the second one (risk management) is not in place, then achieving compliance becomes irrelevant and probably cannot be meaningfully achieved. There are different software tools or "GRC platforms" for tracking and managing GRC activities across the organization. Vendors like SAP and Oracle have embedded the governance, risk, and compliance application suite with their ERP applications. These suites manage risk and compliance across an organization by creating a centralized hub of risk and compliance documentation, assessments, analyses, and loss information from related parts of the business. As opposed to integrated ERP applications that may have some components of a GRC application suite built into the business process, there are other applications also available that focus mainly on GRC activities monitoring. ControlPath® and Risk Navigator® applications are examples of such monitoring software.

ControlPath®

The ControlPath Compliance Suite is a specially designed solution for enterprise risk management and compliance. It has a security controls knowledgebase, a robust workflow, and enterprise risk reporting capabilities to enable it in complying with self-assessment and automated management of remediation actions and controls testing. It has a library of more than 2,000 controls, which simplifies the creation of policies and the mapping of compliance regulations. The ControlPath solution has an automated compliance process that allows organizations to leverage their compliance work efforts across multiple regulations like Sarbanes-Oxley and the Health Insurance Portability and Accountability Act (HIPAA). ControlPath enables organizations to cost-effectively comply with regulatory requirements, while managing and reducing enterprise risk. ControlPath's Compliance Suite also contains enhanced reporting capabilities and automatic assessment questionnaires using a program management module. It also provides each user with a customized management dashboard, allowing them to focus on the charts, graphs, and compliance messages that apply to different individuals.

Risk Navigator®

Risk Navigator is a platform for regulatory compliance and operational risk management. Risk Navigator is a configurable solution that establishes organizationwide accountability to support ongoing compliance demands. The product's role-based security functionality safely distributes responsibilities and allows information to be appropriately shared through ad hoc reporting capabilities. Risk Navigator also can be used for control self-assessment surveys. It is a flexible platform that can evolve to meet changing regulatory and organizational requirements. Risk Navigator supports operational risk management by:

- Identifying and scoring enterprisewide risks based on significance and likelihood.
- Identifying controls and rating relationships to each risk.
- Allowing management to set targeted risk standards.

Risk Navigator can:

- Measure variance versus target risks and prioritize based on criticality.
- Identify issues and track action plans and owners.

Chapter 10: Automated Tools: Using Technology to Audit

- Monitor progress against goals.
- Customize all views and reports for internal use and reporting.

Precautions

Before and during the use of automated tools to assist in the audit process, an IT auditor should generally undertake some precautions to maintain the accuracy of results, security of confidential information, and integrity of data. Some concerns are enumerated below:

- Before selecting any automated tool, an IT auditor must obtain reasonable assurance of its integrity, reliability, and usefulness.

- The IT auditor should conduct a cost-benefit analysis before selecting any automated tool. Automated tools should only be used if the benefits derived by using them outweigh the cost incurred.

- Before using a tool for extracting information for data analysis, the IT auditor must confirm the integrity of the information system and IT environment from which the data is to be extracted.

- When an automated tool is used to extract sensitive information or production data that requires confidentiality to be maintained, the IT auditor must adhere to the organization's data classification and data handling policies to appropriately safeguard the requisite information and production data.

- If an automated tool is installed in an environment that is not under the control of the IT auditor, adequate controls should be implemented to prevent and detect changes to it.

Section IV
Presenting a Technology Audit

IIA Standard 2400 – Communicating Results
Internal auditors must communicate the engagement results.

2410 – Criteria for Communicating
Communications must include the engagement's objectives and scope as well as applicable conclusions, recommendations, and action plans.

> **2410.A1** – Final communication of engagement results must, where appropriate, contain internal auditors' overall opinion and/or conclusions.

> **2410.A2** – Internal auditors are encouraged to acknowledge satisfactory performance in engagement communications.

> **2410.A3** – When releasing engagement results to parties outside the organization, the communication must include limitations on distribution and use of the results.

> **2410.C1** – Communication of the progress and results of consulting engagements will vary in form and content depending upon the nature of the engagement and the needs of the client.

2420 – Quality of Communications
Communications must be accurate, objective, clear, concise, constructive, complete, and timely.

Interpretation:
Accurate communications are free from errors and distortions and are faithful to the underlying facts. Objective communications are fair, impartial, and unbiased and are the result of a fair-minded and balanced assessment of all relevant facts and circumstances. Clear communications are easily understood and logical, avoiding unnecessary technical language and providing all significant and relevant information. Concise communications are to the point and avoid unnecessary elaboration, superfluous detail,

redundancy, and wordiness. Constructive communications are helpful to the engagement client and the organization and lead to improvements where needed. Complete communications lack nothing that is essential to the target audience and include all significant and relevant information and observations to support recommendations and conclusions. Timely communications are opportune and expedient, depending on the significance of the issue, allowing management to take appropriate corrective action.

2421 – Errors and Omissions
If a final communication contains a significant error or omission, the chief audit executive must communicate corrected information to all parties who received the original communication.

2430 – Use of "Conducted in Conformance with the *International Standards for the Professional Practice of Internal Auditing*"
Internal auditors may report that their engagements are "conducted in conformance with the *International Standards for the Professional Practice of Internal Auditing*," only if the results of the quality assurance and improvement program support the statement.

2431 – Engagement Disclosure of Nonconformance
When nonconformance with the Definition of Internal Auditing, the Code of Ethics, or the *Standards* impacts a specific engagement, communication of the results must disclose the:

- Principle or rule of conduct of the Code of Ethics or Standard(s) with which full conformance was not achieved;
- Reason(s) for nonconformance; and
- Impact of nonconformance on the engagement and the communicated engagement results.

2440 – Disseminating Results
The chief audit executive must communicate results to the appropriate parties.

Interpretation:
The chief audit executive or designee reviews and approves the final engagement communication before issuance and decides to whom and how it will be disseminated.

2440.A1 – The chief audit executive is responsible for communicating the final results to parties who can ensure that the results are given due consideration.

2440.A2 – If not otherwise mandated by legal, statutory, or regulatory requirements, prior to releasing results to parties outside the organization the chief audit executive must:

- Assess the potential risk to the organization;
- Consult with senior management and/or legal counsel as appropriate; and
- Control dissemination by restricting the use of the results.

2440.C1 – The chief audit executive is responsible for communicating the final results of consulting engagements to clients.

2440.C2 – During consulting engagements, governance, risk management, and control issues may be identified. Whenever these issues are significant to the organization, they must be communicated to senior management and the board.

CHAPTER 11

INTERPRETING AUDIT RESULTS

An internal audit engagement includes testing control activities and assessing whether the control activities have been designed adequately and are operating effectively to meet the specific internal control assertions. Control activities that are identified as not adequately designed or not operating effectively are noted as observations by the internal auditor. These observations are further analyzed to make recommendations that can mitigate the potential risks posed by the specific control weaknesses.

The strategic value of internal auditing is realized only when the results of the audit procedures are interpreted to include significant risk exposures, control issues, and governance issues at the organization level rather than at just the control activity level. To communicate the audit engagement outcomes effectively, interpretation of audit results is the core of the process. To identify the overall enterprise risk and be able to make recommendations that can mitigate these risks, the internal auditor should be able to identify repetitive groupings/patterns of observations that indicate higher-level issues.

The internal auditor should evaluate the factors affecting each observation relative to the cause, its impact, its likelihood, and the way in which it is affecting the mitigation of risk and use judgment in determining the impact of all of the observations when taken into perspective (aggregated). These issues may not be technology related or may be outside the purview of the IT function; however, they can be relevant in terms of business continuity planning and succession planning.

For instance, an audit engagement may result in three or four observations with none of those constituting a significant observation; however, when taken together, they may constitute a significant observation. The following illustration may help in understanding the concept clearly:

ABC organization uses different financial applications for different purposes like raw material procurement, account payables management, account receivables management, sales recording, and inventory management. The auditors observed that in one of the applications used for procurement, a user named "P" has access privileges in excess of what is required to perform his job. This observation, when analyzed on a standalone basis, may not result in a significant observation. However, if it is observed that the same user has privileges in excess of his role in payables and inventory management application, this may amount to a significant observation.

The following is a general frame of reference that can be helpful when considering the significance of observations An individual observation, or group of observations, is considered insignificant if the control activity in question has a remote likelihood (slight chance) of failing or the impact of its failure is inconsequential (trivial). A significant observation refers to an individual observation, or group of observations, if the control activity in question has a more than remote likelihood of failing or the impact of its failure is more than inconsequential. However each audit function should have a consistent set of definitions used across all audits, including IT, and defined by the needs of the organization.

The internal auditor should confirm all the preliminary facts and observations with appropriate management representatives of the audited department before they are communicated in final form as an audit report. This is usually accomplished through a formal meeting referred to as an "exit interview" or "closing conference" with the management. As part of the exit interview, the internal audit function meets with the individuals from the audited department and evaluates agreement with the preliminary findings and observations discussed throughout the engagement. This process provides an opportunity for all the parties involved to review what is anticipated to be presented in the final audit report and resolve any misunderstandings.

Exit interviews also provide the management of the audited department with an opportunity to present their thoughts and planned actions regarding the observations to be covered in the final audit report. Management's action plan to address and resolve control weaknesses identified during the audit engagement forms part of the management's response section of the report. These corrective action plans are formulated with the recommendations from the internal audit function, but are ultimately the responsibility of the management to implement. Most internal audit engagements include management's response in the final formal communication or audit report.

CHAPTER 12

WRITING THE AUDIT REPORT

Communication is an integral part of an assurance engagement and it occurs on an ongoing basis throughout the span of the engagement. The results of the engagement are generally communicated using various forms of communication that include memoranda, face-to-face meetings, conference calls, and draft working papers. The purpose of these communications is to discuss the observations as they are identified during the engagement. This helps in ascertaining that the facts are accurate and in initiating a dialogue regarding the best method to mitigate the identified observations.

The information gathered during these interim communications is used to finalize the observations that will go into the final engagement communication, referred to as the audit report. An audit report is the formal communication to provide the audit results to the management and other appropriate parties, as well as serve as a record of the work performed.

The audit report is the final element of the audit process. It communicates the results of the audit work to management and facilitates management's efforts to take corrective action to address any identified control weaknesses. Writing an effective audit report requires a clear understanding of the audience and how the report will be used, viewed, and acted upon by the department subject to the audit and management.

Audit reports typically have three major objectives:

- Inform: To provide information to justify the implementation of actions.
- Persuade: To persuade the management to take necessary actions.
- Record: To serve as a record of the audit and its results.

Internal auditors serve as the eyes and ears of the board and/or management. Therefore, one of the key services they provide back to their clients is information with which they might not otherwise have been aware. Based on the interpretation of that information, the auditor attempts to persuade management to address the identified issues through the identification of associated risks, potential impacts, possible remediation, etc. Finally, the auditors record the audit procedures and results in the audit report for communicating to clients and for future reference.

Structure of an Audit Report

The structure of an audit report typically consists of a cover letter followed by:

- Heading.
- Executive Summary.
- Audit Objective (Purpose).
- Audit Scope.
- Audit Opinion.
- Comments (Observations).
- Recommendations.

The following sections may also be part of the audit report:

- Confidentiality Note.
- Management Response.

Heading: The heading should typically include the name of the organization, the location and department audited, and date of the report.

Executive Summary: This section should include a brief summary of the entire report, including the audit objective and scope, comments, recommendations, and details of the team that performed the audit.

Audit Objective (Purpose): This section should describe the objectives of the audit engagement and may, where necessary, inform the recipient/reader why the project was conducted and what it was expected to achieve.

Audit Scope: This section should identify the client activities that were subject to the engagement and include, where appropriate, supportive information, such as the time period covered by the engagement. Related client activities not covered by the project should be identified, if necessary, to delineate the boundaries of the project. Documenting what was not in scope helps to clearly identify the limits of the audit. The nature and extent of procedures performed also should be described.

Audit Conclusion: This section should give an overview of the effects of observations and recommendations. It puts the observations in perspective based on the overall implications. This can include the auditors' evaluation of whether the activities under review are functioning as intended and the organization's goals are being met, and acknowledge satisfactory performance.

Comments (Observations): This section should include the condition, criteria, cause, and effect of the weaknesses noted. Comments also may be referred to as findings or observations. This section also may include improvements made by the client since the previous engagement to provide an appropriate perspective and balance to the report.

Recommendations: This section of the report is used by the auditors to propose to management an approach for potential improvements and corrective actions needed to mitigate risks and achieve the desired results.

Other details may include:

Confidentiality Note: A note that defines the intended recipients of the report and the approval levels required to release the report to external parties.

Management Response: Refers to the advance review and comments of responsible clients (management) and others, as may be appropriate for each observation made by the auditors. Including management observations for the observations made by the auditors makes the audit report fair and complete by adding the perspective of not only what was found and what the auditors think about it, but also what the responsible persons think about it (concurrence or non-concurrence), what they plan to do about it (action plan), when it will be addressed (timeline with target dates), and by whom (responsible party).

Know Your Audience

The audit report may be read by different audience groups or audit customers and should generally be structured to cater to the information needs of each audience group without overwhelming any of them with unnecessary or additional information. The audit customers typically use the report to identify the action steps from the perspective of the scope of their role in the organization and the level of detail presented in the report should be customized. To provide the maximum benefit from a technology audit, it is necessary to understand management's expectations for the purpose and operation of the internal control activities in the context of the business as a whole, and provide clear linkages between those expectations and the results of the audit. In other words, know your audience and design the output of the audit to match their level of strategic concern, operational need, and technological knowledge. This frequently means that several different reports will need to be developed for various entities and individuals within an organization to most effectively communicate the results of an audit in a meaningful and understandable manner.

The primary audience for an IT audit report can be categorized as:

- Technical management.
- Senior management/audit committee.
- Third party.

Technical Management

Technical management is the executive(s) responsible for the audited business unit. They are the process owners and implementers of the audited processes. They have the responsibility to take action in response to the audit findings. Their actions to mitigate risks are directly based on the observations and recommendations of the audit report.

This group views the audit report to understand:

- The particular processes or activities that require their attention.
- The risks identified.
- The necessary actions required to mitigate the risks.

Technical management audit customers are familiar with the day-to-day operational context of the unit. The audit report should have details that can translate the recommendations into actions to improve the effectiveness and efficiency of the audited processes and activities.

Refer to Appendix 1 for a sample detailed audit report.

Senior Management/Audit Committee

Senior management or audit committee members are the high-level decision makers about the strategy and resources for the audited business unit. They are responsible for ensuring that the control environment of the business unit is effective and the corporate governance is maintained. They are interested in identifying the trends in risks and the management of the risks from the insights provided in the observations and recommendations of the audit report.

This group views the audit report to understand:

- What are the risks identified?
- Why do the risks exist?
- What is the severity of the risk exposure?
- How are risks being managed?

These audit customers are not always familiar with the day-to-day operational context of the business unit. Hence, they are interested in knowing that actions are being taken to address the risks but not the actual details of the actions. To this group of audit customers, the audit report observations should have details of the cause and effect of the risks identified and the recommendations should highlight the actions that can mitigate the risks. Whereas line management and the employees responsible for the day-to-day reliability and functioning of specific control activities need detailed results of an audit to understand their operating effectiveness and formulate remediation programs when necessary, upper management wants to understand the bigger picture. It is important to keep in mind that it is not the relative success or failure of individual control activities with which management is primarily concerned, but rather the achievement of control objectives and the impact on the business that senior managers and the board of directors are most interested in.

Refer to Appendix 2 for a sample high-level audit report.

Third Party

A third-party audience for an audit report can include external auditors, key suppliers, and key customers. The audit report observations and recommendations can affect the third parties in their scope of work (external audit) or their relationship (key suppliers and customers) with the organization.

This group typically views the audit report to understand:

- What are the risks identified?
- What is the cause of the risk?
- What are the recommendations?
- What is management's response?

This third-party audience wants to understand the details behind the high-level risk issues.

Language and Presentation

An audit report is a tool to communicate the audit procedures and results of the audit work and serves as a record for future reference. Hence, apart from being accurate, objective, and timely, it should be clear, concise, constructive, and complete. While accuracy, objectivity, and timeliness of an audit report are outcomes of the audit procedures followed, being clear, concise, constructive, and complete are outcomes of the writing quality.

Following are some guidelines that can help in writing an audit report that is clear, concise, constructive, and complete:

Clear: A report is clear when the audience can find the information they need easily. The structure of the report should be logical and the sentence construction readable.

- Keep the length of sentences to an average of 15–20 words.
- Use facts and figures to convey ideas.
- Avoid unfamiliar jargon and acronyms.
- Avoid qualifiers and generalizations.
- Follow grammar for the sentence structure.

Concise: A concise report conveys all that is needed to be conveyed without overwhelming the audience with too much information.

- Convey the message first and then the conditions of the message.
- Avoid explaining in detail the conditions with which the audience is already familiar.

Chapter 12: Writing the Audit Report

- Use graphs, pictures, etc., wherever feasible.

Constructive: A constructive report persuades the audience to take action without getting defensive about the audit observations and recommendations.

- Maintain a balance in presenting the amount of positive and negative information to match the actual message being conveyed.
- Avoid words with strong negative connotation.
- Acknowledge the positive performance of controls as well.

Complete: A complete report not only presents the audit observations and audit opinion, it also focuses on presenting recommendations that are actionable.

- Include condition, criteria, cause, effect, and recommendation for every audit message.
- Make sure recommendations are actionable.
- Make sure all the audit procedures followed have been recorded in the report.

Delivering Findings to an Audit Committee

Audit committees may include executives who have authority over the subject matter but are involved indirectly in the audit procedures that led to the audit report. This group of users is generally more interested in understanding the findings of the audit procedures to be able to make decisions about issues regarding the control environment and corporate governance.

Audit findings can be delivered in the form of summarized reports/executive summaries or as oral presentations accompanied by PowerPoint slides to the audit committee members to facilitate fast decision-making and in the interest of best using the time that the audit committee members can devote to the audit report.

Following are some tips that can help in preparing summarized reports and oral presentations:

Executive Summary: The executive summary should stand alone to communicate the findings of audit procedures and should be comprehensive enough to capture all the important elements of the audit procedures that support the findings. Identify clearly what needs to be conveyed to the audit committee that can trigger action and:

- State the specific objectives of the executive summary.
- Ensure the title and subtitles are concise and meaningful.
- Focus on key messages that are important for the audit committee.
- Describe the risk issues clearly and concisely.
- Use facts and figures to support the messages.
- Be constructive in presenting the positive and negative messages.
- Include the recommendation to address the issues identified.
- Make sure all the objectives mentioned are addressed.
- Check the format, grammar, language consistency, and spelling.

Oral Presentation: Oral presentation is an interactive mode of communicating the findings of audit procedures and is usually accompanied by PowerPoint slides. The information conveyed is the same as in an executive summary and requires a design approach that keeps in mind all the guidelines mentioned above.

PowerPoint slides should facilitate the oral discussion and include information that highlights the key elements of the discussion points. The slides should present only the talking points, not the entire report. Following are some additional guidelines to help in preparing PowerPoint slides for the oral presentation:

- *Titles of the slides:* Use meaningful and compelling captions.
- *Key messages:* Present one idea per slide.
- *Six-six rule:* Follow a six-six rule — a slide should not contain more than six lines or bullet points and each line should not have more than six words.
- *Visual appeal:* Use a font size that is legible and color schemes that are visually appealing.
- *Facts and figures:* Use appropriate metrics and figures to convey the key messages.
- *Handouts:* Use handouts to provide reference material to the audience.

APPENDIX 1

SAMPLE DETAILED AUDIT REPORT

INTERNAL AUDIT REPORT

ABC Corporation
<Department>
Information Technology Audit

EXECUTIVE SUMMARY x
AUDIT OBJECTIVE AND SCOPE x
AUDIT CONCLUSION x

AUDIT DETAIL REPORT x
SCOPE x
APPROACH x
RESULTS x
AUDIT REPORT FORMAT x

AUDIT COMMENTS AND RECOMMENDATIONS FOR ITS x
APPLICATION 1 x
    A. APPLICATION 1 USER ACCESS ADMINISTRATION
       PROCESS x
    B. ADMINISTRATIVE ACCESS IN APPLICATION 1 x
    C. ACCESS TO APPLICATION 1 ADMIN MODULE x
    D. DEVELOPERS' ACCESS TO DIRECTORIES ON PRODUCTION
       SERVER x
APPLICATION 2 x
    A. APPLICATION 2 USER ACCESS ADMINISTRATION PROCESS x
    B. DESIGN OF USER PROFILES IN APPLICATION 2 x
    C. APPLICATION 2 USER ACCESS AND PASSWORD PARAMETER
       CONFIGURATION x
    D. APPLICATION 2 APPLICATION SERVER USER
       ACCESS x
    E. APPLICATION 2 GATEWAY SERVER USER ACCESS
       AND PASSWORD CONFIG x

AUDIT COMMENTS AND RECOMMENDATIONS FOR
BUSINESS UNITS x
APPLICATION 1 x
    A. APPLICATION SECURITY AND SEGREGATION
       OF DUTIES x

Appendix 1: Sample Detailed Audit Report

EXECUTIVE SUMMARY

Objectives

The audit objective was to review the nature of Information Technology Services' internal controls and its ability to meet business objectives. Our goal is to ascertain whether controls to protect the IT applications are in place and are operating effectively.

Scope

The scope of this audit included audit of two applications — Application 1 and Application 2. The audit areas included: Application Security and Segregation of Duties, Database and Operating System Security, and Processing Controls (Exception Reporting, Input Controls, and Activity Logging).

Conclusion

Based on the results of the audit procedures performed, for Application 1 and Application 2, controls surrounding processing controls appear adequate; however, certain controls and procedures related to application security and segregation of duties, database and operating system security, data management, and technology change management need improvement.

AUDIT OF ITS

The Internal Audit Department of ABC Corporation performed an IT audit of two applications supported by Information Technology Services (ITS). The purpose of this audit was to ascertain whether controls to protect these applications are in place and operating effectively. Our audit scope included the following applications:

- **Application 1:** Provides users with the ability to view and research client holdings compared to the custodian holdings.
- **Application 2:** Used to exchange information and communicate with custodians, brokers, and dealers.

The matrix below lists the applications and the audit areas that were tested for each application.

	Applications	
Audit Areas* ***See below for description of audit areas**	**Application 1**	**Application 2**
Application Security and Segregation of Duties	X	X
Database and Operating System Security	X	X
Processing Controls (Exception Reporting, Input Controls, Activity Logging)	X	X

Audit Area Descriptions:

Application Security and Segregation of Duties — To ascertain whether access to applications is restricted in accordance with job responsibilities and allows for adequate segregation of duties.

Database and Operating System Security — To ascertain whether access to the database and the operating systems supporting the in-scope application is restricted in accordance with job responsibilities.

Appendix 1: Sample Detailed Audit Report

Processing Controls (Exception Reporting, Input Controls, and Activity Logging) — To ascertain whether ITS has established adequate processing controls, including: exception reporting, audit and activity logging, and validation controls for input to the application.

The risk areas were identified by internal auditing based on discussions with members of ITS, the Capital Management Team, and the Investment Operations Team. The audit approach involved interviewing management and other key personnel, reviewing policies, procedures, and other applicable documentation, and performing relevant audit procedures of system controls.

Based on the results of the audit procedures performed, the following is our opinion:

- o **Application 1 and Application 2:** Controls surrounding processing controls appear adequate; however, certain controls and procedures related to application security and segregation of duties, database and operating system security, data management, and technology change management need improvement.

REPORT FORMAT

The Audit Comments and Recommendations section of the audit report for the ITS audit has been divided into the following sections:

- o **Audit Comments and Recommendations for ITS:** This section lists the observations relating to controls and processes implemented by ITS. ITS management is responsible for evaluating and implementing corrective actions relating to this section of the report.

- o **Audit Comments and Recommendations for Business Units (Capital Management and Investment Operations):** This section includes observations relating to the Application 1, and it is the responsibility of the business units, Capital Management and Investment Operations, to respond to the comments and recommendations documented in this section of the report. The business units, Capital Management and Investment operations, should work with ITS management to evaluate and implement corrective actions relating to this section of the report.

APPLICATION I

A. Application 1 User Access Administration Process:

The internal audit department noted that the procedures for granting access to the Application 1 application do not appear to promote adequate security control, as noted below:
- o Access request forms indicating Application 1 business owner approval are not documented for granting access to the Application 1 application (through the Portfolio Management View application).
- o Termination and modification controls are not in place to proactively remove users from the Application 1 application timely when an employee changes job functions or is terminated from the organization.
- o Management approved policies and procedures for account provisioning have not been documented to provide consistent guidance for such activities.

Lack of documented policies and procedures for administering access to the Application 1 application and failure to document approval evidence can lead to unauthorized access to the application and inconsistency in security administration processes, including account creation and deletion.

User IDs that are not deleted or modified timely increase the risk of unauthorized access to application, which may lead to manipulation of production data or occurrence of fraudulent activity.

Recommendation:

The internal audit department recommends that ITS management develop policies and procedures for user administration, including creating and deleting user IDs for the Application 1 application. Requests for access to the Application 1 application should be approved via an access request form, and documented approval evidence should be retained.

Appendix 1: Sample Detailed Audit Report

Management Response:

We concur with the observation; however, the finding was a result of the timing of the audit fieldwork. A project to enhance existing documented policies and procedures addressing user provisioning and management was begun last quarter by the IT department at the request of the board and is due to be completed by the end of next month.

B. **Administrative Access in Application 1:**

The internal audit department noted that access to perform administrative activities in Application 1 via the xx_admin profile is not restricted in accordance with job responsibilities. The xx_admin profile provides access to change the Application 1 system configuration parameters in production and should be restricted to only individuals responsible for performing administrative activities within Application 1. There are seven individuals within the ITS group with access to the xx_admin profile in the Application 1 application; however, three out of the seven individuals are not authorized for such access.

Inappropriate access to the xx_admin access level increases the risk of unauthorized changes to the production Application 1, which may lead to inaccurate data and impact the daily reconciliation performed by the business.

Recommendation:

The internal audit department recommends that ITS management restrict access to the xx_admin profile to the Application 1 application administrators based on job responsibilities, and remove user IDs for individuals who do not require such access. Additionally, ITS management should perform periodic reviews of user access to the xx_admin profile for appropriateness.

Management Response:

We concur with the observation. IT Operations will review all users with administrative access to the application immediately and identify those with unnecessary access by the end of the week. All unnecessary accounts will be locked at that time and observed for one month. If no need for the accounts is identified during that time, they will be removed from the system the following week.

C. Access to Application 1 Admin Module:

The internal audit department noted that access to perform Application 1 related account-provisioning activities, including creation and modification of user access via the Admin Module, is not restricted in accordance with job responsibilities. There are 14 individuals with access to the Admin Module in Application 1; however, 11 of them are not authorized for such access.

Unauthorized access to the Application 1 Admin Module increases the risk of inappropriate account provisioning and the creation and/or modification of user access on the Application 1 system. This level of access could compromise data integrity and cause unintentional errors, fraudulent activity, and segregation of duties issues.

Recommendation:

The internal audit department recommends ITS management review the list of users who have access to the Portfolio Management View Admin Module and remove access for unauthorized users. Additionally, ITS management should perform periodic reviews of user access to the Portfolio Management View Admin module for appropriateness.

Management Response:

We concur with the observation; however, the recommendation cannot be implemented by the IT Department. Responsibility for administration of the application is maintained by the business unit, and the users identified without authorization are all employees of the business unit. The three users with authorization are employees of the IT Department and are responsible only for periodic maintenance of the application.

Appendix 1: Sample Detailed Audit Report

D. Developers' Access to Application 1 Directories on Production Servers:

The internal audit department noted that the "develop" group has full access (read, write, and execute) to certain files and subdirectories in 12 out of the 13 Application 1 directories on the P1 and P2 production servers.

Development group permissions ("develop group") on the Application 1 production directories should be restricted to read-only to prevent developers from changing the production Application 1. Access levels such as read, write, and execute are established for different levels of authorization to protect data and systems from inappropriate changes.

Recommendation:

The internal audit department recommends that ITS management review the group-level permissions on the Application 1 directories and files stored on production servers, and remove write permissions from the "develop" group. ITS management should restrict developers from having write access on production servers in the future.

Management Response:

We concur with the observation. The suggested recommendation was implemented immediately upon identification during the course of the audit and the issue is now closed.

APPLICATION 2

A. Application 2 User Access Administration Process:

The internal audit department noted that policies and procedures for account provisioning in the Application 2 Alliance Access software do not exist. Evidence of user access approval for Application 2 users is not documented consistently, and the approval documentation is not retained. Additionally, we noted that there is no process for identifying users that have been terminated from the organization or who have changed job functions.

Lack of policies and procedures for administering access to the Application 2 Alliance Access application and failure to document approval evidence can lead to unauthorized access to the application and inconsistency in security administration processes, including account creation and deletion.

Recommendation:

The internal audit department recommends that ITS management develop policies and procedures for user administration, including creation and deletion of user IDs for the Application 2 Alliance Access application, and these procedures should be consistently followed. Requests for user access to the Application 2 should be approved, and documented approval evidence should be retained by the security administrators.

Management Response:

We concur with the observation. A project to develop policies and procedures applicable to Application 2 will be initiated in conjunction with the associated business unit management at the close of Q3. Final documentation will be submitted jointly by the IT Department and the business units to management for approval by the end of Q4.

B. **Design of User Profiles in Application 2:**

The internal audit department noted that user profiles (access levels) in Application 2 are not designed to appropriately restrict access based on job responsibilities, as noted below:

Profile Superkey: This profile is designated for system administrators; however, it should not have access to the X1 Management application, which should be restricted to Application 2 Business Analysts for appropriate segregation of duties. Additionally, this profile has access to create and authorize all types of Application 2 messages; however, because this profile is designed for system administrators, the profile should be restricted from creating business critical messages, such as FIN31 and FIN32, etc.

Appendix 1: Sample Detailed Audit Report

Application Message Modification: This application allows users to modify messages within the Application 2. Access to modify messages should be restricted to business users (Asset Management) who are authorized to create such messages. The system and application administrators should not have access to Message Modification application, as it is not required based on their job responsibilities.

The current design of the Superkey profiles does not enforce appropriate segregation of duties, as the Superkey profile has access to all Application 2. If access to the X1 Management application is not restricted appropriately, there is an increased risk of transmission of X1 and the exchange of critical trade messages with custodians not authorized to do business with ABC Corporation. Additionally, failure to restrict application administrators from creating and authorizing financial (FIN) messages increases the risk of the exchange of unauthorized FIN messages, and could lead to fraud.

Access to the Message Modification application in the Application 2 Alliance Access application can lead to unauthorized modification of messages received from or delivered to custodians.

Recommendation:

The internal audit department recommends that ITS management review the current setup for profiles in the Application 2 and restrict Superkey profiles from access to the X1 Management application, and restrict the transmission of business critical messages. Additionally, the application Message Modification should be restricted to users who need such access to perform their job responsibilities. ITS management should review the setup of other profiles in Application 2 and restrict access for appropriate segregation of duties.

Management Response:

We concur with the observation. Currently the application as provided by the vendor is limited in the configurable parameters for the Superkey profile and cannot be modified. Discussions with the vendor indicate that changes to the software are due with the next version upgrade scheduled for early next year, which will allow implementation of the suggested recommendation. In the interim, all access to, and use of, the Superkey profile will be logged and monitored by the security department. The issue will be investigated once the next upgrade is implemented.

C.   **Application 2 User Access and Password Parameter Configuration:**

Application 2 User Access:

The internal audit department noted that access to the Application 2 Alliance Access application is not restricted appropriately, as noted below:

- We noted four user IDs that belong to terminated employees (Person A, Person B, Person C, Person D).
- We noted two users (Person X and Person Y) who do not have responsibilities related to the Application 2 application; therefore, their access is not consistent in accordance with job responsibilities.
- We noted eight generic user IDs in the Application 2 Alliance Access application; however, business justification for six of the eight user IDs was not available. These user IDs are: User1, User2, User3, User4, User5, and User6.

Failure to restrict user access to the Application 2 Alliance Access application to active employees in accordance with job responsibilities increases the risk of unauthorized access and manipulation of production data. This condition may lead to fraud, abuse, or disruption of service.

Existence of user IDs that cannot be associated to unique individuals or that do not have business justification does not establish appropriate accountability to a specific user. This circumstance increases the risk of unauthorized access to servers and manipulation of data or programs that cannot be traced to a specific user.

Application 2 Password Parameter Configuration:

The internal audit department noted that password parameters in the Application 2 Alliance Access application are not configured in accordance with the ABC Corporation User ID and Password Policy, as noted below:

Appendix 1: Sample Detailed Audit Report

Account locked threshold is set to 0 (recommended setting of three (3). Password complexity is not enabled (password complexity should be enabled).

Passwords control logical access to the application; and failure to configure password controls in a secure manner increases the risk of an individual gaining inappropriate access to the application.

Recommendation:

The internal audit department recommends that ITS management perform a review of user access to the Application 2 Alliance Access application and remove terminated users, users who do not require access to the application in accordance with their job responsibilities, and generic user IDs that do not have business justifications. Additionally, ITS management should perform periodic reviews of user access to the application to maintain access integrity.

The internal audit department recommends that ITS management configure the following password parameters in the Application 2 Alliance Access application to comply with the ABC Corporation User ID and Password Policy:
  - *o   Account lockout threshold is to be set to three (3) attempts.*
  - *o   Password complexity is enabled.*

Management Response:

We concur with the observation. The suggested recommendation was implemented immediately upon identification during the course of the audit and the issue is now closed.

D. **Application 2 Application Server User Access:**

The internal audit department noted the following user access-related issues in the application server for the Application 2 Alliance Access software:

  - o   User access is not restricted in accordance with job responsibilities. The Information Systems' network support group consists of users who are not members of the ABC Corporation network

support group; however, these users have administrative access to the server.
- o Developers have administrative access in this server via the Information Systems engineers group.
- o The "Administrator" (super-user) account, which is a generic account and does not belong to a unique individual, has not been disabled.

Failure to restrict user access in accordance with job responsibilities increases the risk of unauthorized access, manipulation of production data, and implementation of unapproved changes in the server. In addition, developers' access to production servers creates segregation of duties issues.

Existence of privileged user IDs that cannot be associated to unique individuals does not establish appropriate accountability to a specific user. This circumstance increases the risk of unauthorized access to servers and manipulation of data or programs that cannot be traced to a specific user.

Recommendation:

The internal audit department recommends that ITS management perform a review of access to the server and remove inappropriate users. ITS management should solicit the help of security administration, network support, and the database administration teams to recertify the list of users who require access to these servers.

The default "administrator" account should be deleted and uniquely identifiable user accounts should be used to establish accountability. Additionally, management should develop a process to perform periodic reviews of user access to privileged accounts (administrator accounts).

Management Response:

We concur with the observation. All users without a need to access the system were removed during the course of the audit. The administrator account cannot be removed; however, it was disabled and individual accounts were created for IT personnel. Documented procedures for user access reviews

Appendix 1: Sample Detailed Audit Report

will be developed by the IT Department and submitted to management for approval by the end of the month.

E. **Application 2 Gateway Server User Access and Password Configuration:**

Application 2 Gateway Server User Access
The internal audit department noted the following user access host server issues for the Application 2 Gateway:

The "Administrator" (super-user) account, which is a generic account and does not belong to a unique individual, has not been disabled. Four user IDs — "X," "Y," "J," and "K" — belong to terminated employees.

Existence of privileged user IDs that cannot be associated to unique individuals does not establish appropriate accountability to a specific user. This circumstance increases the risk of unauthorized access to servers and manipulation of data or programs that cannot be traced to a specific user.

Failure to restrict user access to active employees in accordance with job responsibilities increases the risk of unauthorized access, manipulation of production data, and implementation of incorrect changes in the server.

Application 2 Gateway Server Password Configuration
The internal audit department noted that the password parameters in the server are not configured in accordance with the ABC Corporation User ID and Password Policy, as noted below:

Password expiration is set to 42 days, instead of 30 days, as required. Account lockout threshold is set to five (5) attempts, instead of three (3) attempts, as required.

Passwords control logical access to the server and failure to configure password controls in a secure manner increases the risk of an individual gaining unauthorized access to the application.

Recommendation:

The internal audit department recommends that ITS management perform a review of access to the server and remove the inappropriate users. Access to this server should be restricted to the Application 2 administrators. The default "administrator" account should be deleted and uniquely identifiable user accounts should be used to establish accountability. Additionally, management should consider developing a process to perform a periodic review of user access to privileged accounts (administrator accounts).

The internal audit department recommends that ITS management configure the following password parameters in the Application 2 Alliance Access application to comply with the User ID and Password Policy:
- *o   Passwords are to be set to expire every 30 days.*
- *o   Account lockout threshold is to be set to three (3) attempts.*

Management Response:

We concur with the observation. All users without a need to access the system were removed during the course of the audit. The administrator account cannot be removed; however, it was disabled and individual accounts created for IT personnel. Documented procedures for user access reviews will be developed by the IT Department and submitted to management for approval by the end of the month. Passwords in accordance with the recommended values were implemented during the course of the audit and the issue is now closed.

BUSINESS UNIT OBSERVATIONS

A.   Application 1 User Access for Capital Management and Wealth Management:

The internal audit department noted that access to the Application 1 application (for Wealth Management and Capital Management instances) was not restricted appropriately, as noted below:

Appendix 1: Sample Detailed Audit Report

WEALTH MANAGEMENT:

User access (update) and clearance levels for 33 out of 81 users in the Wealth Management Application 1 environment are not consistent in accordance with job responsibilities:
Two (2) user IDs — "J" and "R" — in Application 1 belong to terminated employees.
Four (4) user IDs — "K," "M," "Y," and "N" — have multiple profiles in Application 1.

CAPITAL MANAGEMENT:

User access (update) levels for 33 out of 46 users in the Capital Management Application 1 environment are not consistent in accordance with job responsibilities.

Note: For the purposes of this audit, the internal audit department did not inspect users with read-only access in the Application 1 application due to the low risk associated with this level of access.

Recommendation:

The internal audit department recommends that Capital Management and Investment Operations management perform a review of user access to the Application 1 for Capital Management and Wealth Management environments, and request ITS management to remove user IDs or update access levels of individuals consistent with their job responsibilities. Additionally, management from the business units should develop a process to perform a periodic review of user access to the Application 1.

Management Response:

We concur with the observation. The IT Department will work with the responsible business units under the direction of management to develop and implement appropriate processes.

APPENDIX 2

SAMPLE HIGH-LEVEL AUDIT REPORT

Sample Corporation

Internal Audit Report
(Name of Audit)

(Date of Report Issuance)

The Sample Corporation

Internal Audit Report
(Name of Audit)

We have completed an internal audit of the _____ function. Our testing covered the period _____ through _____. Our internal audit was directed toward determining whether the processes for controlling _____ are adequately designed and operating effectively.

Our report is organized in two sections. The Executive Summary section of this report provides an overview of the _____ and highlights our major concerns and resulting recommendations. The Comments and Recommendations section further discusses the significant issues disclosed by our work.

Based on the results of our testing, we conclude that the controlling processes over _____ (are adequate/need strengthening/are inadequate). Consequently, we rate this area as "_____." (See Appendix I for a definition of the report ratings.)

Appendix 2: Sample High-level Audit Report

EXECUTIVE SUMMARY

Background:

Our testing covered the period _____ through _____, and included _____.

The "_____" rating was based on the fact that existing policies (do not) provide an adequately designed framework for the controlling processes. To provide assurance that both management objectives are met and internal controls operate in an effective manner, we recommend management:

-
-
-
-

COMMENTS AND RECOMMENDATIONS

1. (Title of Comment):

Condition, Criteria, Cause, Effect, and Recommendation of Comment.

Management Response:

Appendix 2: Sample High-level Audit Report

APPENDIX A

(NAME OF AUDIT)
INTERNAL AUDIT CONCLUSIONS

Internal auditing is an independent appraisal activity within the corporation. Its primary objective is to review, test, evaluate, and report on the adequacy and effectiveness of control systems.

At the conclusion of audit projects, internal auditors report on an exception basis to appropriate levels of management for corrective action. These reports are routed to senior management and summarized for the audit committee of the board of directors who have requested that audit reports come to overall conclusions.

Therefore, the Internal Audit Department has established the practice of drawing an overall conclusion on internal control adequacy in each report as follows:

Satisfactory — The level of internal controls is functioning effectively. This covers effectiveness and efficiency of operations, reliability of accounting records, compliance with applicable laws and regulations, appropriate supervision, and compliance with policies and procedures. If audit concerns are noted, they are considered minor in nature.

Needs Improvement — The level of internal controls, effectiveness and efficiency of operations, reliability of accounting records, compliance with applicable laws and regulations, supervision, or compliance with policies needs to be improved. Either the volume or the relative significance of the audit concerns noted requires positive action.

Unsatisfactory — Internal control systems are not functioning as intended. Some examples include: noncompliance with significant policies, lack of supervision, deficient accounting records and documentation, or previously cited weaknesses that are still present. The condition requires some basic improvements with more than usual management involvement and monitoring until controls are improved.

APPENDIX 3

ADDITIONAL READING AND RELATED RESOURCES

This section contains references, brief descriptions, and links to useful material not cited in the body of the work that can be helpful to an IT auditor in learning about or performing IT audits.

The IIA's Audit Reference Library: http://www.theiia.org/ITAuditArchive/index.cfm?act=ITAudit.reflib.

COSO's *Enterprise Risk Management – Integrated Framework* from the Committee of Sponsoring Organizations of the Treadway Commission. http://www.coso.org.

Center for Internet Security (CIS): http://www.cisecurity.org.

Institute for Security and Open Methodologies (ISECOM): http://www.isecom.org.

Open-Source Security Testing Methodology Manual (OSSTMM 2.1): http://www.isecom.org/osstmm.

SysAdmin, Audit, Network, Security Institute (SANS): http://www.sans.org.

Computer Security Resource Center of the National Institute of Science and Technology (NIST): http://csrc.nist.gov.

TCP/IP Illustrated Volume 1: The Protocols (W. Richard Stevens, Addison-Wesley Professional, 1994).

TCP/IP Illustrated Volume 2: The Implementation (W. Richard Stevens, Addison-Wesley Professional, 1995).

APPENDIX 4

CONTRIBUTORS

Writers

Nelson Gibbs (Lead Author), CIA, CISA, CISSP, CISM, CGEIT
Divakar Jain, CA, CPA, CISA
Amitesh Joshi, CA, CISA
Surekha Muddamsetti
Sarabjot Singh, CIA, CISA

Contributing Editors

Nelson Gibbs (Lead Editor), CIA, CISA, CISM, CGEIT, CISSP
Sarah Adams, CISA
Gerald Canon, CISA
Carey Carpenter, CPA, CISA
Harry Hong, CISSP
Michael Juergens, CIA, CISA, CGAP, CGEIT,
Sara Lademan, CIA, CISA, CISSP, CGEIT
Deborah Luskin, CISA, CISSP
David Maberry, CRP
Neil Marano, CISA, CISSP
David Melnick, CISA, CISSP
Monica O'Reilly, CGEIT
YC Zhu, CISA

BIBLIOGRAPHY/REFERENCES

The Institute of Internal Auditors' Publications

1. *The International Professional Practices Framework;* IIARF (2009).
2. *Systems Auditability & Control;* IIARF (1994).
3. *Systems Assurance & Control;* IIARF (2002).
4. Critical Infrastructure Assurance Project:
   a. *Information Security Management & Assurance: A Call for Corporate Governance;* The IIA (2000).
   b. *Information Security Governance: What Directors Need to Know;* The IIA (2001).
   c. *Building, Managing, and Auditing Information Security;* The IIA (2001).
5. *Internal Auditing: Assurance & Consulting Services;* Redding, et al.; IIARF (2007).
6. *Internal Auditing: The Practice of Modern Internal Auditing;* Sawyer, et al; IIARF (2005).
7. *Designing and Writing Message-based Reports;* Cutler, IIARF (2001).
8. *Use of Information Technology in Auditing;* LeGrand, ITAudit Forum (2002).
9. *An e-Risk Primer;* Parker, IIARF (2001).
10. *Audit Committee Effectiveness: What Works Best,* 3rd ed.; PWC, IIARF (2005).
11. Global Technology Audit Guide series (vol. 1-13); The IIA (2005–2009):
    a. *Information Technology Controls.*
    b. *Change and Patch Management Controls: Critical for Organizational Success.*
    c. *Continuous Auditing: Implications for Assurance, Monitoring, and Risk Assessment.*
    d. *Management of IT Auditing.*
    e. *Managing and Auditing Privacy Risks.*
    f. *Managing and Auditing IT Vulnerabilities.*
    g. *Information Technology Outsourcing.*
    h. *Auditing Application Controls.*
    i. *Identity and Access Management.*
    j. *Business Continuity Management.*

k. *Developing an IT Audit Plan.*
l. *Auditing IT Projects.*
m. *Fraud Prevention and Detection in an Automated World.*
12. *GAIT: Guide to the Assessment of IT General Controls Scope Based on Risk.*

ISACA Publications

1. *IS Standards, Guidelines & Procedures for Auditing and Control Professionals;* ISACA (2007).
2. *CobiT 4.1;* ITGI (2007).
3. *CobiT Security Baseline;* ITGI (Second Edition, 2007).
4. *Val IT,* ITGI (2006).
5. *Risk IT,* ITGI (2009).
6. *IT Assurance Guide: Using COBIT,* ITGI (2007).
7. *Information Security Harmonization – Classification of Global Guidance* (2005).

Deloitte & Touche Publications

1. *eCommerce Security: Enterprise Best Practices;* ISACF (2000).
2. *eCommerce Security: Securing the Network;* ISACF (2002).
3. *eCommerce Security: Business Continuity Planning;* ISACF (2002).

Miscellaneous Publications

1. *Internal Control – Integrated Framework;* COSO (1994).
2. *Auditing Information Systems,* 2nd ed.; Champlain, Wiley & Sons (2003).
3. *Tell It to the CEO;* Maniak, Skills-Builder Press (2005).
4. *Information Security Oversight: Essential Board Practices;* KPMG, National Association of Corporate Directors (2001).
5. *Securing eBusiness Systems: 0A Guide for Managers & Executives;* Braithwaite, Wiley & Sons (2002).
6. *IT Auditing: The Process;* Davis, Pleier Corp. (2005).
7. *IT Auditing: The Basics;* Lapelosa, Pleier Corp. (2005).
8. *Auditing IT Infrastructures;* Oliphant, Pleier Corp. (2004) .

Bibliography/References

Periodicals

1. *Information Systems Control Journal;* ISACA [various: vol 4 (2002) – vol 4 (2007)].
2. *Internal Auditor;* The IIA (various: June 2005 – August 2007).
3. *IEEE Security & Privacy* (various: vol. 1, #1 – vol. 2, #1).
4. *ISSA Journal* (various).

IIA/Deloitte Technology Training Seminars

1. "Introduction to IT Auditing."
2. "IT Auditing: Beyond the Basics."
3. "Information Security Concepts."
4. "Internet Security for IT Auditors."